CW00469305

Bricks Without Mortar

HARTLEY COLERIDGE (1796–1849), poet and essayist, was the eldest of Samuel Taylor Coleridge's three children. Aside from his time at university at Oxford and a few years in London and Leeds, he spent most of his uneventful, eccentric life in the Lake District. Only one volume of his poetry was published during his lifetime.

LISA GEE lives in London and works as a freelance journalist, lecturer, website editor and literary publicist. She is currently researching a biography of William Hayley.

Bricks
Without Mortar

The selected poems of Hartley Coleridge

Edited by Lisa Gee

PICADOR

First published 2000 by Picador
an imprint of Macmillan Publishers Ltd
25 Eccleston Place, London SW1W 9NF
Basingstoke and Oxford
Associated companies throughout the world
www.macmillan.com

ISBN 0 333 48044 8

1 3 5 7 9 8 6 4 2

A CIP catalogue record for this book is available from
the British Library.

Typeset by SetSystems Ltd, Saffron Walden, Essex
Printed and bound in Great Britain by
Mackays of Chatham plc, Chatham, Kent

FOR MY FAMILY,

IN THE BROADEST SENSE

ACKNOWLEDGEMENTS

Thanks to: Louis de Bernierès; Charles Cox; Graham Davidson; Mary Mount; Don Paterson; Adam Rae-Reeves; Roger Robinson; Stevie Taylor; Dr Brian Wells; Robert Woof and his colleagues at Dove Cottage; and the Trustees of the Wordsworth Trust, Dove Cottage, Grasmere for permission to use Sir David Wilkie's portrait of Hartley as the front cover illustration and for allowing me to quote from Harriette Harrison's journal.

Foreword *by Louis de Bernières*

Hartley Coleridge was in some ways an archetypal genius; he was eccentric without actually being mad, he was compulsively creative, he was passionately intelligent, and the exigencies of life failed to make him sensible or to damp his productive ardour. He had both a childlike nature and a very sophisticated ability to examine things from an interested distance.

It is inevitable that he should have been compared to his father, whose verbal brilliance he shared, but it is in my opinion quite mistaken. In some of his knottier poems one detects a debt both to John Donne and to Shakespeare, but it seems obvious to me that his real poetic parent is the young William Wordsworth, and it is clear from some of his poems that he had an affection for folk song. Much of his work achieves in full measure the project set out in *Lyrical Ballads*, and he himself was exactly the child of nature that Wordsworth once wished himself to be.

Wordsworth's poetry eventually declined into a kind of garrulous conservatism, and Samuel Taylor Coleridge made the mistake, unfortunately very common in writers, of thinking that he could be a philosopher. Apart from opium addiction, I cannot think of anything more deleterious to the poetic spirit than the study of German Idealists such as Kant and Fichte, whose literary style ought to have been a capital offence, and whose ideas about perception inevitably led to a kind of paralysing solipsism. Only Schopenhauer could actually write beautifully, and he came on the scene too late to save Samuel Taylor Coleridge from the abyss. Hartley was indeed interested in the major issues, but he addressed them directly and plainly, and thus rather more effectively than his father did.

Hartley could not help being a writer, and one of the distinct joys of reading him is to be infected by the obvious delight that he took in writing. His poetry is full of music, space and light, and these spaces are themselves full of the poet's pleasure. His poetry is conceptual rather than visual, and it is with great honesty and humility that the poet reveals his own sense of unworthiness, his sense of isolation, his resigned and wistful longing for love, his fear that there might be no purpose to life, and the apprehension of the painful and irretrievable losses wrought by the passage of time. These poems can be very touching, but we do not become depressed because the poet has taken pleasure in the telling of it, and always there is another poem which is life-affirming and celebratory, whose humour and lightness of touch sets up the necessary balance.

There are some lovely poems in this collection, poems that will stay with the reader for a long time afterwards. It would be easy to yield to the temptation to tell the reader which ones I think they are, but I shall resist it. I say, find out for yourself. Put Samuel Taylor Coleridge out of your mind for a while, and read Hartley as if he were somebody else's son.

Introduction

According to his friend and former pupil Thomas Blackburne, Hartley Coleridge's 'favourite spot was a little glade above Stock-gill force, quite shut in with trees and hills, where the stream flows in deep lucid pools. "I wonder what pleasure the people find in that noisy fall," he one day said to me, "I like this silence a great deal better; but no one notices it." '[1] And such has been the fate of his poetry. Even during his lifetime, Hartley's verse – at its best gently, lucidly perfect – was drowned out by the Niagara of his father's virtuosity, and since then, it has been overshadowed by Samuel Taylor Coleridge's seemingly unassailable centrality to the poetic canon. Nonetheless, he persisted in his vocation, even though no one was listening.

It was Don Paterson – poet and Picador's poetry editor – who first drew my attention to Hartley Coleridge; he was researching another anthology and found himself captivated by the few samples of Hartley's work that he uncovered. He showed these to me, and I set off to investigate whether they were representative of the larger body of Hartley's writing, or if they were rare gems shining amidst an otherwise muddy mediocrity. This selection of the best of Hartley Coleridge's poetry is the result. Spelling and punctuation follow the 1833 volume of Hartley's verse – the only one to be published in his lifetime – and the posthumous collection edited by his younger brother Derwent. Where there are differences between the two, I've kept to the 1833 text, except on a couple of occasions where Derwent's punctuation was

---

1. Derwent Coleridge (ed.), *Poems by Hartley Coleridge: With a Memoir of his Life by his Brother*, vol.I, p.cxxxv.

clearly more careful and correct than his brother's. The title of this collection was drawn from one of Hartley's numerous (unpublished) notebooks: 'Bricks without Mortar from the Tower of Babel'.

Hartley Coleridge's poetic ambition is utterly different from his father's, and probably best summed up in the following lines from 'A Task Ad Libitum':

> . . . the humbler spirit
> Hears in the daily round of household things
> A low sweet melody, inaudible
> To the gross sense of worldlings.[2]

We are, I believe, accustomed to the idea of poetry making us see things differently. But what Hartley Coleridge aims to do is something that is at once subtler and also perhaps more difficult. He wants to make us *listen* differently: to encourage us to appreciate silence, to hear the low sweet melodies we miss amongst the everyday clatter; the nearby, small beauties that escape our field of vision when we train our focus only on the highest mountains and the deepest rivers. He is, in essence, a poet of the ear rather than of the eye. And this, inevitably, has implications for his subject matter:

> . . . Aye I grant
> That earth and sky are cunning instruments;
> But who may rouse their sleeping harmony,
> And not torment the strings to grinding discord,

---

2. These lines allude to Wordsworth's 'Lines written a few miles above Tintern Abbey': 'The still, sad music of humanity'.

> Or vex the hearers with the weary drone
> Of half-forgotten lays,

and means his aims and ambitions are also very different from those of his contemporaries Keats, Shelley and Byron. What Hartley gives us is an unadulterated appreciation and celebration of the domestic and the feminine, surprising – if not unique – in a nineteenth-century male writer. His oeuvre breathes democracy rather than preaching it, and manifests a quiet critique of colonial practices and values that seems disconcertingly modern. And all this combines with a self-mocking introspection seemingly devoid of egotism. 'No hope have I', he wrote in 'Poietes Apoietes', 'to live a deathless name,'

> Not mine the skill in memorable phrase,
>   The hidden truths of passion to reveal,
> To bring to light the intermingling ways,
>   By which unconscious motives darkling steal:
>
> To show how forms the sentient heart affect,
>   How thoughts and feelings mutually combine,
> How oft the pure, impassive intellect
>   Shares the mischances of his mortal shrine.

And in his essay *The Books of My Childhood*, he claimed: 'I was a great storyteller, but my stories were never original. Whatever I heard or read, I worked up into a tale of my own, in which there was no invention of incident, but sometimes great circumstantiality of description, and something like an attempt at character. I had always an intense feeling of beauty.'[3] His priorities, then, are different from Samuel Taylor Coleridge's and Keats's privileging

---

3. *Essays and Marginalia*, p.346.

of the imagination, and his sensibility more closely akin to Wordsworth's than to his father's. But the sheer delicacy of description is entirely his own (the nearest comparison is probably with a poet writing now – John Burnside). These lines from 'Let me not deem that I was made in vain'

> The very shadow of an insect's wing
> For which the violet cared not while it stay'd
> Yet felt the lighter for its vanishing
> Proved that the sun was shining by its shade:

demonstrate his capacity for noticing the unnoticeable, and for rendering concrete and precise the intangible. And in 'Night', he takes us deep into the silence of rural night by detailing the absence of those background noises that we would, commonly, remain unconscious of. He achieves this partially through using hushed, sibilant language – 'embers', 'still', 'sill', 'small birds', 'voiceless flowers', 'shed' and so on, so that the words themselves say 'shhh':

> The crackling embers on the hearth are dead;
> The indoor note of industry is still;
> The latch is fast; upon the window sill
> The small birds wait not for their daily bread;
> The voiceless flowers—how quietly they shed
> Their nightly odours;

There is, however, a vast disparity between Hartley Coleridge's best and his worst work. He wrote a great deal, especially later in life, when he was known for popping into whichever cottage he was passing, grabbing pen and paper and jotting down a quick verse (Burns, who shared this effortless facility, had a similar habit). When asked for his autograph, he would often oblige with an impromptu sonnet. And most of this considerable output – much of which is still sloshing around in manuscript (a few months ago I picked up a signed original for a mere £45) – is of poor quality. Alcohol accounts for some of the weaknesses, low self-esteem, hurried composition and lack of editing for others –

> He never kneaded, or pounded his thoughts; they always came out *cap-à-pie*, like a troop in quick march. To see him brandishing his pen . . . and now and then beating time with his foot, and breaking out into a shout at any felicitous idea, was a thing never to be forgotten. The common method of keeping up the velocity, by muttering and re-muttering what is written, and using one line as a spring-board to reach another, was not the method which he adopted. His sonnets were all written instantaneously, and never, to my knowledge, occupied more than ten minutes . . .[4]

– and a whimsical sentimentality that, to a millennial sensibility, feels just a little twee, for the rest. Where his verse is bad it's truly terrible (although it is fair to bear in mind that much of this stuff was never intended for public consumption). But his good work is absolutely of the first water. Take Sonnet XXVIII 'To Shakspeare' (see p. 19). Shakespearean in its perfection, this poem is also reminiscent of the fifth of John Donne's 'Holy Sonnets' ('I am a little world made cunningly / Of elements'). Here, Hartley – seemingly without effort – transports the reader between unimaginable vastness and the safety of the ark, between busy, fecund creativity and Zen-like calm; his language throughout deceptively simple, his use of imagery precise, inconspicuous and utterly effective.

---

4. Derwent Coleridge (ed.), *Poems by Hartley Coleridge*, vol.I, p.cxxxiii.

There are dark and weighty preoccupations at the core of Hartley's poetry. Take the lines 'Let me not deem that I was made in vain, / Or that my Being was an accident', the sonnet that commences

> It were a state too terrible for man,
> Too terrible and strange, and most unmeet,
> To look into himself, his state to scan,
> And find no precedent, no chart, or plan,
> But think himself an embryo incomplete,
> Else a remnant of a world effete,
> Some by-blow of the universal Pan,
> Great nature's waif, that must by law escheat
> To the liege-lord Corruption.

and the conclusion to 'Stay Where Thou Art':

> May God in mercy from thy knowledge hide
> All but the path in which thou art advancing.
> For evil things there are, on either side,
> Dark flames on one, like antic demons dancing,
> And on the left a desert waste and wide,
> Where is no chart, no compass, and no guide.

and the frequent references to 'the vast, void sky', 'the abysmal dark / Of the unfathom'd centre', 'the dark abyss / Of time', all of which suggest that in writing, as in life, the poet is fighting to escape the pull of a black hole. A desperate need for each and every life – even his – to have meaning, is articulated against the fear that religion might prove empty rhetoric rather than absolute truth.

But woven into this watered silk of dark, empty fears and bright, fractured beliefs, are Hartley's hopes and prayers:

So have I dream'd! — oh, may the dream be true! —
That praying souls are purged from mortal hue,
And grow as pure as He to whom they pray.

[from 'There is an awful quiet in the air']

There is a fable, that I once did read,
Of a bad angel, that was someway good,
And therefore on the brink of Heaven he stood,
Looking each way, and no way could proceed;
Till at last he purged away his sin
By loving all the joy he saw within.

[from 'How shall a man fore-doom'd to lone estate']

and most plainly and beautifully in the final two lines of 'Multum
Dilexit' – the last poem (according to Derwent) that Hartley ever
wrote, extraordinary for its clear-eyed ingenuousness.

I am a sinner, full of doubts and fears,
Make me a humble thing of love and tears.

Hartley wasn't always so earnest. He was also capable of a self-
deprecating humour – although it invariably tended towards the
gallows. In 'To a Cat', for instance, which commences

Nelly, methinks, 'twixt thee and me,
There is a kind of sympathy;
And could we interchange our nature, —
If I were cat, thou human creature, —
I should, like thee, be no great mouser,
And thou, like me, no great composer;

and concludes

The world would just the same go round
If I were hang'd and thou wert drown'd;

There is one difference, 'tis true,—
Thou dost not know it, and I do.

And just occasionally, he'd turn his humour – although gently and respectfully – towards someone else. Sonnet XXXIV, for instance, 'To a Lofty Beauty, from her Poor Kinsman', where he writes teasingly of how, had he not watched her grow up, heard her 'baby cries' and watched her 'girlish, sweet vicissitude', he'd be terrified of his cousin, Edith (Southey's daughter), because her combination of 'scornful mood, / And bearing high of stately womanhood' tyrannizes 'O'er humble love'. Or in the ditty 'Lines', which starts

If I were young as I have been,
And you were only gay sixteen,
I would address you as a goddess,
Write loyal cantos to your boddice,

and continues

But I am old, and you, my fair,
Are somewhat older than you were.
A lover's language in your hearing
Would sound like irony and jeering.

which might not have been altogether appreciated by the poem's subject ... if she ever got to see it (which, given Hartley's propensity for undeclared and, therefore, unrequited love, seems highly unlikely).

Next to the perfection of its music – his poetry is seldom, if ever, discordant – perhaps the most striking quality Hartley Coleridge's writing possesses is its unassumingly democratic spirit. This never manifests through preaching, but rather seems to breathe through the poems as a natural, unquestioned part of their – and their author's – constitution. And, as contemporary accounts of Hartley indicate (see the biographical sketch at the end of this book), he was a genuine egalitarian, widely respected by the Lakespeople for the way he treated all men and women as equals, never talking down to anyone. He proved time and time again that he was as ready to share his thoughts and ideas with them as he was to listen to their concerns, or help care for and play with their children. In the notes to the 1833 collection of his verse he makes explicit the sources of all the allusions in his poems – from Cædmon to Wordsworth – demonstrating that he wasn't writing only for an intellectual elite who would automatically recognize the references, but also for a wider, less comprehensively educated audience.

Alongside his sonnet 'To the Memory of Canning',[5] the two poems that present the most unequivocal statements of Hartley's political credo are 'The Dandelion' and the long, unfinished poem 'Prometheus'. The former of these, another sonnet, provides an oblique yet precise critique of colonialism. Here, Hartley muses on the 'Strange plants we bring from lands where Caffirs roam', describing how the explorer 'That can inflict his queer and ugly name / On product of South Afric sands or loam', which he transplants into the glass-housed collection of some English aristocrat, will achieve great 'botanic fame', before proceeding to hope that

> . . . Haply time may be
> When botanist from fire-born Owhyhee
> Shall bear thee, milky mother of white down,

---

5. George Canning (1770–1827), British statesman, foreign secretary and, for the four months before his death, prime minister, who supported the working classes and promoted electoral reform.

Back to his isle, a golden gift superb; —
Give name uncouth to diuretic herb,
And from the Dandelion reap renown.

What seems to be implied here is a desire for the traffic of both knowledge (Hartley stated clearly that 'Knowledge is power when in the possession of a powerful mind',[6] and it's evident that he believed powerful minds were to be found in all races and classes) *and* wealth – the Dandelion is, after all, 'a *golden* gift' (my italics) – to flow both ways, rather than simply transfer from 'South Afric sands or loam' to the English 'lordly garden'.

Composed at around the same time (one of significant grass-roots political unrest in England) that Shelley was writing 'Prometheus Unbound', but never completed,[7] Hartley's 'Prometheus' is astonishing for its political – and poetic – subtlety. Shelley's 'Prometheus Unbound' records a simple struggle between the extremes of good and evil, between two immortals: the great, enabling hero and prophet (Prometheus), who gave fire – and encouragement – to Mankind, and the tyrannical god Jove, who punished Prometheus for his egalitarianism, so seeking to defend the status quo and to keep the people in their place. And the poem uses the pyrotechnic language of extremes combined with martial rhythms. Take this stanza from the Song of Spirits (Act II, Scene iii):

While the sound, whirls around,
        Down, down!
As the fawn draws the hound,
As the lightening the vapour,

---

6. In his essay *A Preface That May Serve For All Modern Works of the Imagination.*
7. Perhaps because Hartley read Shelley's work?

As a weak moth the taper;
Death, Despair; Love, Sorrow;
Time both; to-day, to-morrow;
As steel obeys the Spirit of the stone,
Down, down!

(Note how Shelley hammily overemphasizes the vigour of the rhythm by inserting a superfluous comma after the internal rhyme in the first line.)

Hartley's take on this battle of wills is dramatically different. In his 'Prometheus', the eponymous protagonist is a far from unblemished character – he is proud and it's his arrogance, as much as Jove's wrath, which precipitates his punishment. And Jove is not all bad. Yes, he's a tyrant much given to throwing his weight around – mostly in the form of thunderbolts – but unlike Shelley's villain, he's not beyond redemption. Thus, unsurprisingly, Hartley's language and rhythms are correspondingly gentler. Hartley's Prometheus gets to articulate his fair share of 'Death, Despair ... Sorrow'. However, the chorus of Sylphs playing opposite him,[8] speaks with a quiet, butter-mild voice, light with the softness of each individual spirit and infused with their synergic harmonies.

'Prometheus' Hartley-style is perhaps most noteworthy for the sophisticated, ahead-of-its-time treatment of power, its configuration and location. In Shelley's 'Prometheus Unbound' power equals might, physical strength, and hence is the prerogative of the suffering hero Prometheus and the tyrannical anti-hero Jove. In Hartley's poem, power – quite literally – resides in the grass

---

8. Itself an interesting choice, demonstrating that we're not dealing with a straight Prometheus–Jove, hero–anti-hero dichotomy.

roots, in the rosebuds, in the streams and in the woods: and everywhere else, in the formless multitude of Sylphs, who explain to Prometheus how 'There is a spell of unresisted power / In wonder-working simplicity, / Because it is not fear'd.' Which means that Jove will listen to and obey their quiet, small voices:

> . . . Time hath been ere now
> That Jove hath listen'd to our minstrelsy,
> Till wrath would seem to drop out of his soul
> Like a forgotten thing. Our smallest note,
> Catching his ear at any breathing space
> Amid his loudest threats, would make him mute
> As wondering childhood. True, the fault is great,
> But we are many that will plead for thee;

Prometheus's exaggerated sense of his own power and importance are demonstrated in his concern that if the Sylphs plead for him before Jove, they'll be punished:

> . . . Gentle powers, forbear!
> 'Twere worse than all my former miseries
> Should my huge wreck suck down the friendly skiff
> That proffer'd aidance.

A little later, however, he appears to realize his mistake – neither he nor Jove has the power to destroy these incorporeal creatures:

> You, at least,
> Have nought to fear. Your unsubstantial forms
> Present no scope to the keen thunderbolt;
> Nor adamant can bind your subtle essence,
> Which is as fine as scent of violets,
> Quick as the warbled notes of melody,
> And unconfinable as thoughts of gods.

The Sylphs, then, wield supreme power in Hartley Coleridge's version of the Prometheus myth paradoxically *because* of their lack of individual might. Ultimately, the tough individualistic *Sturm und Drang* of gods and heroes is no match for their collective gentleness: the destructive capabilities of masculine strength are – inevitably and appropriately – overpowered by a soothing feminine persistence.

Whilst Hartley's tendency to idealize women is obvious, for instance, when he writes at the close of 'A Task Ad Libitum'

> And should I sing of thee and thy soft brilliance,
> Thy tender thoughts, in reckless laughter melting,
> Thy beautiful soul, that shapes thine outward form
> To its own image, — thy essential goodness,
> Not thine, but thee, — thy very being's being,
> Thy liquid movements, measured by the notes
> Of thy sweet spirit's music, the unearthly sound
> Of that beloved voice, less heard than felt,
> That wins the wayward heart to peace, and lulls
> The inmost nature to that blissful sleep
> Which is awake to heaven, and brings no dream,
> But foretaste of the best reality:
> Then must I moderate empyreal ether
> To strains more sweet than mortal sense could bear.

the fact that a concept of feminine power permeates his work arguably bespeaks a nascent feminism – a willingness, at least, to listen to and respect women and their strengths that is lacking in the work of his immediate precursors and contemporaries who, even where they preach gender equality – as Shelley is famous for doing – do so from a pulpit of assumed superiority, in language as solipsistically macho as that employed by the average heavy metal band.

Ultimately, all this may amount to is the assertion that Hartley himself was, in some way, feminized, that his work evolved more out of the eighteenth-century culture of Sensibility than early nineteenth-century Romanticism. Be that as it may, he was a poet who listened in an era of preachers – a writer who used his work to describe and elucidate, rather than to express himself, at a time when poems were supposed to leap, like Athena from Zeus' forehead, fully-formed from the troubled, imagination-harrowed brow of the poet. There's something hugely touching in his evident belief in the redemptive power of love – 'And He wiped off the soiling of despair / From her sweet soul, because she loved so much' ('Multum Dilexit') – and a gorgeous, hypnotic sweetness in the gentle, simple language and rhythms he wraps it all up in. In the sheer ordinariness of much of his subject matter, he seems so much more at home than Wordsworth did when trying to 'ascertain how far the language of conversation in the middle and lower classes of society is adapted to the purposes of poetic pleasure'.[9] No one – least of all the man himself – would consider Hartley Coleridge the brightest star in the literary firmament of nineteenth-century Romanticism. But he is a major poet, whose soft brilliance, low, sweet melodies and spark of earthly fire, draw us into a quiet, strong current where we can swim in the silence he held so dear.

---

9. From advertisement to *Lyrical Ballads*, 1798.

Bricks Without Mortar

Long Time a Child . . .

Long time a child, and still a child, when years
Had painted manhood on my cheek, was I;
For yet I lived like one not born to die;
A thriftless prodigal of smiles and tears,
No hope I needed, and I knew no fears.
But sleep, though sweet, is only sleep, and waking,
I waked to sleep no more, at once o'ertaking
The vanguard of my age, with all arrears
Of duty on my back. Nor child, nor man,
Nor youth, nor sage, I find my head is grey,
For I have lost the race I never ran,
A rathe December blights my lagging May;
And still I am a child, tho' I be old,
Time is my debtor for my years untold.

How Long I Sail'd

How long I sail'd, and never took a thought
To what port I was bound! Secure as sleep,
I dwelt upon the bosom of the deep
And perilous sea. And though my ship was fraught
With rare and precious fancies, jewels brought
From fairy-land, no course I cared to keep,
Nor changeful wind nor tide I heeded ought,
But joy'd to feel the merry billows leap,
And watch the sun-beams dallying with the waves;
Or haply dream what realms beneath may lie
Where the clear ocean is an emerald sky,
And mermaids warble in their coral caves,
Yet vainly woo me to their secret home;
And sweet it were for ever so to roam.

Song

The earliest wish I ever knew
Was woman's kind regard to win;
I felt it long e're passion grew,
E'er such a wish could be a sin.

And still it lasts;—the yearning ache
No cure has found, no comfort known:
If she did love, 'twas for my sake,
She could not love me for her own.

The First Birth Day

The Sun, sweet girl, hath run his year-long race
Through the vast nothing of the eternal sky—
Since the glad hearing of the first faint cry
Announc'd a stranger from the unknown place
Of unborn souls. How blank was then the face,
How uninform'd the weak light-shunning eye,
That wept and saw not. Poor mortality
Begins to mourn before it knows its case,
Prophetic in its ignorance. But soon
The hospitalities of earth engage
The banish'd spirit in its new exile—
Pass some few changes of the fickle Moon,
The merry babe has learn'd its Mother's smile,
Its father's frown, its nurse's mimic rage.

To an Infant

Sure 'tis a holy and a healing thought
That fills my heart and mind at sight of thee,
Thou purest abstract of humanity.
Sweet infant, we might deem thy smile was brought
From some far distant Paradise, where nought
Forbad to hope whate'er of good may be,
Where thou could'st know, and feel, and trust, and see
That innocence which, lost, is vainly sought
In this poor world. Yet, if thou wert so good
As love conceives thee, thou hadst ne'er been born;
For sure the Lord of Justice never would
Have doomed a loyal spirit to be shorn
Of its immortal glories—never could
Exile perfection to an earth forlorn.

A Task Ad Libitum

To a Lady

You bid me write, and yet propose no theme.
Must I then shoot my shafts of poesy
At the vast, void, invulnerable air?
Or lead my Pegasus a steeple-hunting?
Or issue forth with chiming hue and cry,
With trampling feet of thorough-paced blank verse
And winding horn of long-drawn melody
In chase of butterflies? Or shall I rather,
In gentler figure, *make believe* to hang
My careless harp upon a willow tree,
That every gale may prattle with its strings?
'Tis strange that any bard should lack a theme
In such a world of wonders. Look abroad,
Around you, and above you, and within you:
The stars of heaven (as elder sages told)
Roll on from age to age their lonely way
To their own music. So the humbler spirit
Hears in the daily round of household things
A low sweet melody, inaudible
To the gross sense of worldlings.—Aye, I grant
That earth and sky are cunning instruments;
But who may rouse their sleeping harmony,
And not torment the strings to grinding discord,
Or vex the hearers with the weary drone
Of half-forgotten lays, like buzzing night-flies,
Thwarting the drowsiness themselves produce?
All, all is stale: the busy ways of men,

The gorgeous terrors of the steel-clad warrior,
The lover's sighs, the fair one's cruelty,
Or that worst state, when love, a rayless fire,
Is sever'd quite from hope and tenderness,
Or dogg'd by base suspicion, hurries onward,
Scared by its own black shadow.—These are themes
Unmeet for thee, or old, or harsh and strange.
The gentler joys, the calm sequester'd hours
Of wedded life, the babble sweet of babes,
That unknown tongue, which mothers best expound,
Which works such witchery on a parent's heart,
Turning grave manhood into childishness,
Till stoic eyes with foolish rheum o'erflow,
And fluent statesmen lisp again,—for love
Will catch the likeness of the thing beloved,—
These have been sung a thousand times before;
And should I sing of thee and thy soft brilliance,
Thy tender thoughts, in reckless laughter melting,
Thy beautiful soul, that shapes thine outward form
To its own image,—thy essential goodness,
Not thine, but thee,—thy very being's being,
Thy liquid movements, measured by the notes
Of thy sweet spirit's music,—the unearthly sound
Of that beloved voice, less heard than felt,
That wins the wayward heart to peace, and lulls
The inmost nature to that blissful sleep
Which is awake to heaven, and brings no dream,
But foretaste of the best reality:
Then must I moderate empyreal ether
To strains more sweet than mortal sense could bear.

Not in One Clime...

Not in one clime we oped the infant eye
To the blank light of yet unmeaning day;
Nor in one language timely taught to pray,
Did we lisp out the babies' liturgy.
But even then, we both alike did sing
Our joys and sorrows in the self-same way,
Instinct the same sweet native tune did play,
From laugh to smile, from sob to chasten'd sigh,
Our tutor'd spirits were alike subdued.
What wonder, then, if, meeting in this isle,
We eke imperfect speech with sigh and smile,
The catholic speech of infancy renew'd.
True love is still a child, and then most true
When most it talks, and does as children do.

How Shall a Man . . .

How shall a man fore-doom'd to lone estate,
Untimely old, irreverendly grey,
Much like a patch of dusky snow in May,
Dead sleeping in a hollow, all too late—
How shall so poor a thing congratulate
The blest completion of a patient wooing,
Or how commend a younger man for doing
What ne'er to do hath been his fault or fate?
There is a fable, that I once did read,
Of a bad angel, that was someway good,
And therefore on the brink of Heaven he stood,
Looking each way, and no way could proceed;
Till at last he purged away his sin
By loving all the joy he saw within.

It Must Be So . . .

It must be so,—my infant love must find
In my own breast a cradle and a grave;
Like a rich jewel hid beneath the wave,
Or rebel spirit bound within the rind
Of some old wreathed oak, or fast enshrined
In the cold durance of an echoing cave:—
Yea, better thus than cold disdain to brave:—
Or worse,—to taint the quiet of that mind,
That decks its temple with unearthly grace.
Together must we dwell, my dream and I,—
Unknown must live, and unlamented die,
Rather than soil the lustre of that face,
Or drive that laughing dimple from its place,
Or heave that white breast with a painful sigh.

How Many Meanings ...

How many meanings may a single sigh
Heave from the bosom; early, yet too late,
I learn'd with sighs to audit mine estate,
While yet I deem'd my hope was only shy
And wishing to be woo'd. Fain to descry
The little cloud I thought could never vex
My vernal season, I would still perplex
With sighs the counsel of my destiny.
Still it moved on, and ever larger grew,
And still I sigh'd and sigh'd—and then I panted;
For now the cloud is huge, and close to view.
It burst; the thunder roar'd, the sharp rain slanted,
The tempest pass'd, and I was almost fain
To sigh forlorn, and hear the sigh again.

To My Unknown Sister-In-Law

Mary, our eyes are strangers, but our hearts
Are knit in active sympathy of love
For one, whom love of thee hath sanctified.
The lawless wanderings of his youthful thought
For thee he curbed—for thee assumed the yoke
Of humble duty—bade the world farewell,
With all its vanities of prose and rhyme—
The secular pride of startling eloquence,
The victory of wordy warfare—all
That charm'd his soul in academic bowers.

Not small the struggle and the sacrifice,
When men of many fancies, daring minds,
That for the substance and the form of truth
Delight to fathom their own bottomless deeps,
Submit to authorised creeds and positive laws—
Appointed rites and ceremonial duty—
And he, the pastor of a christian flock,
That is no hireling drudging at a task
Ungenial, nor intruder, bold and proud,
Unhallow'd, unanointed, self-inspired,
Of all men hath the greatest need of love,
To keep his thoughts, his hopes, his heart at home.—
If human speech have aught of holiness,
'Tis all compris'd in three thrice-holy names
Of Father, Husband, Minister of Christ:—
Or if a holier title yet there be,
That name is Mother.

Dearest sister, I
Am one of whom thou doubtless hast heard much—
Not always well.—My name too oft pronounced
With sighs, despondent sorrow, and reproach,
By lips that fain would praise, and ever bless me.
Yet deem not hardly of me: who best know
Most gently censure me,—and who believes
The dark inherent mystery of sin
Doubts not the will and potency of God
To change, invigorate, and purify
The self-condemning heart.

                 Good night:—e'en now
Perhaps thou art sleeping by my brother's side,
Or listening gladly to the soft, sweet breath
Of thy dear babe—while I must seek a couch
Lonely, and haunted much by visions strange,
And sore perplexity of roving dreams,
The spectres manifold of murdered hours,—
But yet, good night—good be the night to thee,
And bright the morrow:—Once again, good night.

Lines

If I were young as I have been,
And you were only gay sixteen,
I would address you as a goddess,
Write loyal cantos to your boddice,
Wish that I were your cap, your shoe,
Or any thing that's near to you.
But I am old, and you, my fair,
Are somewhat older than you were.
A lover's language in your hearing
Would sound like irony and jeering.
Once you were fair to all that see,
Now you are only fair to me.

I Saw Thee . . .

I saw thee in the beauty of thy spring,
And then I thought how blest the man shall be
That shall persuade thy maiden modesty
To hearken to his fond soliciting.
Thou wert so fair, so exquisite a thing,
I thought the very dust on which thy feet
Had left their mark exhaled a scent more sweet
Than honey-dew dropt from an angel's wing.
I see thee now a matron and a mother,
And I, alas! am old before my day.
Both to myself and thee I owe another—
A holier passion, a devouter lay.
Each spark of earthly fire I now must smother,
And wish for nought for which I dare not pray.

Homer

Far from all measured space, yet clear and plain
As sun at noon, 'a mighty orb of song'
Illumes extremest Heaven. Beyond the throng
Of lesser stars, that rise, and wax, and wane,
The transient rulers of the fickle main,
One steadfast light gleams through the dark, and long,
And narrowing aisle of memory. How strong,
How fortified with all the numerous train
Of human truths, Great Poet of thy kind,
Wert thou, whose verse, capacious as the sea,
And various as the voices of the wind,
Swell'd with the gladness of the battle's glee—
And yet could glorify infirmity,
When Priam wept, or shame-struck Helen pined.

To Shakspeare

The soul of man is larger than the sky,
Deeper than ocean—or the abysmal dark
Of the unfathom'd centre. Like that Ark,
Which in its sacred hold uplifted high,
O'er the drown'd hills, the human family,
And stock reserved of every living kind,
So, in the compass of a single mind,
The seed and pregnant forms in essence lie,
That make all worlds. Great Poet 'twas thy art,
To know thyself, and in thyself to be
Whate'er love, hate, ambition, destiny,
Or the firm, fatal purpose of the heart,
Can make of Man. Yet thou wert still the same,
Serene of thought, unhurt by thy own flame.

On Parting with a Very Pretty, but Very Little Lady

'Tis ever thus. We only meet on earth
That we may know how sad it is to part:
And sad indeed it were, if in the heart,
There were no store reserved against a dearth,
No calmed Elysium for departed Mirth,
Haunted by gentle shadows of past Pleasure;
Where sweet folly, the light-footed measure,
And graver trifles of the shining hearth
Live in their own dear image. Lady fair,
Thy presence in our little vale has been
A visitation of the Fairy Queen,
Who for brief space reveals her beauty rare,
And shews her tricksy feats to mortal eyes,
Then fades into her viewless Paradise.

To a Lofty Beauty,
from Her Poor Kinsman

Fair maid, had I not heard thy baby cries,
Nor seen thy girlish, sweet vicissitude,
Thy mazy motions, striving to elude,
Yet wooing still a parent's watchful eyes,
Thy humours, many as the opal's dyes,
And lovely all;—methinks thy scornful mood,
And bearing high of stately womanhood,—
Thy brow, where Beauty sits to tyrannize
O'er humble love, had made me sadly fear thee;
For never sure was seen a royal bride,
Whose gentleness gave grace to so much pride—
My very thoughts would tremble to be near thee;
But when I see thee at thy father's side,
Old times unqueen thee, and old loves endear thee.

[Written to Mrs Coleridge after Samuel Taylor Coleridge's death]

The silent melody of thought that sings
A ceaseless requiem to the sainted dead;
That so the sharp wound, hid within the heart,
May grow a spot most finely sensible
To each good impress of the hand of God:
Till death no longer seemed a terrible thing,
But like a blithe and long-wished holiday
That frees the spirit weary of the school
And discipline of earth, once more to join
The friends and kindred of their happy home:
While the All-Father, with a look benign,
Praises the task, imperfect though it be,
And blesses all in their love and His own.

Oh! My Dear Mother . . .

Oh! my dear mother, art thou still awake?
Or art thou sleeping on thy Maker's arm,—
Waiting in slumber for the shrill alarm
Ordain'd to give the world its final shake?
Art thou with 'interlunar night' opaque
Clad like a worm while waiting for its wings;
Or doth the shadow of departed things
Dwell on thy soul as on a breezeless lake!
Oh! would that I could see thee in thy heaven
For one brief hour, and know I was forgiven
For all the pain and doubt and rankling shame
Which I have caused to make thee weep or sigh.
Bootless the wish! for where thou are on high,
Sin casts no shadow, sorrow hath no name.

Poietes Apoietes

No hope have I to live a deathless name,
    A power immortal in the world of mind,
A sun to light with intellectual flame,
    The universal soul of human kind.

Not mine the skill in memorable phrase,
    The hidden truths of passion to reveal,
To bring to light the intermingling ways,
    By which unconscious motives darkling steal;

To show how forms the sentient heart affect,
    How thoughts and feelings mutually combine,
How oft the pure, impassive intellect
    Shares the mischances of his mortal shrine.

Nor can I summons from the dark abyss
    Of time, the spirit of forgotten things,
Bestow unfading life on transient bliss—
    Bid memory live with 'healing on its wings.'

Or give a substance to the haunting shades,
    Whose visitation shames the vulgar earth,
Before whose light the ray of morning fades,
    And hollow yearning chills the soul of mirth.

I have no charm to renovate the youth
    Of old authentic dictates of the heart,—
To wash the wrinkles from the face of Truth,
    And out of Nature form creative Art.

Divinest Poesy!—'tis thine to make
Age young—youth old—to baffle tyrant Time,
From antique strains the hoary dust to shake,
And with familiar grace to crown new rhyme.

Long have I loved thee—long have loved in vain,
Yet large the debt my spirit owes to thee,
Thou wreath'd'st my first hours in a rosy chain,
Rocking the cradle of my infancy.

The lovely images of earth and sky
From thee I learn'd within my soul to treasure;
And the strong magic of thy minstrelsy
Charms the world's tempest to a sweet, sad measure.

Nor Fortune's spite—nor hopes that once have been—
Hopes which no power of Fate can give again,—
Not the sad sentence—that my life must wean
From dear domestic joys—nor all the train

Of pregnant ills—and penitential harms
That dog the rear of youth unwisely wasted,
Can dim the lustre of thy stainless charms,
Or sour the sweetness that in thee I tasted.

It Were a State Too Terrible...

It were a state too terrible for man,
Too terrible and strange, and most unmeet,
To look into himself, his state to scan,
And find no precedent, no chart, or plan,
But think himself an embryo incomplete,
Else a remnant of a world effete,
Some by-blow of the universal Pan,
Great nature's waif, that must by law escheat
To the liege-lord Corruption. Sad the case
Of man, who knows not wherefore he was made;
But he that knows the limits of his race
Not runs, but flies, with prosperous winds to aid;
Or if he limps, he knows his path was trod
By saints of old, who knew their way to God.

Let Me Not Deem . . .

Let me not deem that I was made in vain,
Or that my Being was an accident,
Which Fate, in working its sublime intent,
Not wish'd to be, to hinder would not deign.
Each drop uncounted in a storm of rain
Hath its own mission, and is duly sent
To its own leaf or blade, not idly spent
'Mid myriad dimples on the shipless main.
The very shadow of an insect's wing,
For which the violet cared not while it stay'd,
Yet felt the lighter for its vanishing,
Proved that the sun was shining by its shade:
Then can a drop of the eternal spring,
Shadow of living lights, in vain be made?

While I Survey . . .

While I survey the long, and deep, and wide
Expanse of time, the Past with things that were
Throng'd in dark multitude; the Future bare
As the void sky when not a star beside
The thin pale moon is seen; the race that died
While yet the families of earth were rare,
And human kind had but a little share
Of the world's heritage, before me glide
All dim and silent. Now with sterner mien
Heroic shadows, names renown'd in song,
Rush by. And, deck'd with garlands ever green,
In light and music sweep the bards along;
And many a fair, and many a well-known face,
Into the future dive, and blend with empty space.

If I Have Sinn'd . . .

If I have sinn'd in act, I may repent;
If I have err'd in thought, I may disclaim
My silent error, and yet feel no shame—
But if my soul, big with an ill intent,
Guilty in will, by fate be innocent,
Or being bad, yet murmurs at the curse
And incapacity of being worse
That makes my hungry passion still keep Lent
In keen expectance of a Carnival;
Where, in all worlds, that round the sun revolve
And shed their influence on this passive ball,
Abides a power that can my soul absolve?
Could any sin survive, and be forgiven—
One sinful wish would make a hell of heaven.

Humming Birds

The insect birds that suck nectareous juice
From straightest tubes of curly-petaled flowers,
Or catch the honey-dew that falls profuse
Through the soft air, distill'd in viewless showers
Whose colours seem the very souls of gems,
Or parting rays of fading diadems:—

I have but seen their feathers,—that is all.
As much as we can know of poets dead
Or living; but the gilded plumes that fall
Float on the earth, or in the wind dispread
Go everywhere to beautify the breeze.
Sweet wind, surcharged with treasures such as these,

I may not feel:—I never may behold
The spark of life, that trimm'd in garb so bright
That flying quintessence of ruby, gold,
Mild emerald, and lucid chrysolite.
Yet am I glad that life and joy were there,
That the small creature was as blithe as fair.

Who is the Poet?

Who is the Poet? Who the man whose lines
Live in the souls of men like household words?
Whose thought, spontaneous as the song of birds,
With eldest truth coeval, still combines
With each day's product, and like morning shines,
Exempt from age? 'Tis he, and only he,
Who knows that Truth is free, and only free,—
That Virtue, acting in the strict confines
Of positive law, instructs the infant spirit
In its best strength, and proves its mere demerit
Rooted in earth, yet tending to the sky,—
With patient hope surveys the narrow bound,
Culls every flower that loves the lowly ground,
And fraught with sweetness, wings her way on high.

[To a friend]

TO THE SAME

In the great city we are met again,
Where many souls there are, that breathe and die,
Scarce knowing more of nature's potency,
Than what they learn from heat, or cold, or rain,
The sad vicissitude of weary pain:—
For busy man is lord of ear and eye,
And what hath nature, but the vast, void sky,
And the throng'd river toiling to the main?
Oh! say not so, for she shall have her part
In every smile, in every tear that falls;
And she shall hide her in the secret heart,
Where love persuades, and sterner duty calls:
But worse it were than death, or sorrow's smart
To live without a friend within these walls.

CONTINUED

'Tis strange to me, who long have seen no face,
That was not like a book, whose every page
I knew by heart, a kindly common-place—
And faithful record of progressive age—
To wander forth, and view an unknown race;
Of all that I have been, to find no trace,
No footstep of my by-gone pilgrimage.
Thousands I pass, and no one stays his pace
To tell me that the day is fair, or rainy—
Each one his object seeks with anxious chase,
And I have not a common hope with any—
Thus like one drop of oil upon a flood,
In uncommunicating solitude—
Single am I amid the countless many.

In the Manner of a Child of
Seven Years Old

'Tis silly sooth,
And dallies with the innocence of love
Like the old age.

Ah! woe betide my bonny bride,
　　For war is in the land,
And far and wide the foemen ride
　　With ruthless bloody brand.

Still as a dream the purple beam
　　Of eve is on the river,
But ghastly bright, at the dead of night,
　　A blood-red flame will quiver.

Fair in the skies the sun will rise,
　　As ever sun was seen,
But never again our window pane
　　Shall back reflect his sheen:

For the warrior stern our cot will burn,
　　And trample on the bower;
It grew for years of smiles and tears,
　　'Twill perish in an hour.

Those firs were old, our grandsires told,
  In their good fathers' days;
And my soul it grieves that their needle leaves
  Must crackle in the blaze.

Beneath their shade how oft we play'd!
  There was our place of wooing:—
But now we're wed, and peace is fled,
  And we shall see their ruin.

In battle plain shall I be slain,
  And never would I shrink;
Oh! were that all, what may befall
  To thee, I dare not think.

And our sweet boy, our baby joy,
  He'll for his mother cry,
Till the hot smoke, his voice shall choke,
  And then my bird will die.

Green are the graves, and thick as waves,
  Within our holy ground—
And here, and there, an hillock fair,
  An infant's grave is found.

Our fathers died, their whole fireside
    Is laid in peace together,
But, vile as stones, our bleaching bones
    Must brave the wind and weather.

Nay, love, let's fly, to the hill so high,
    Where eagles build their nest,
Among the heather we'll couch together,
    As blithely as the best.

We'll leave the bower and tender flower
    That we have nursed with care;
But the wild blue bell shall bloom as well
    Beside our craggy lair.

We shall not die, for all birds that fly
    Shall thither bring us food,
And come the worst, we'll be help'd the first,
    Before the eagle's brood.

The mist beneath, that curls its wreath
    Around the hill-top hoar,
There will we hide, my bonny bride,
    And ne'er be heard of more.

To the Memory of Canning

Early, but not untimely, Heaven recall'd
To perfect bliss, thy pure, enlighten'd mind;
And tho' the new-born freedom of mankind
Is sick of fear to be again enthrall'd,
Since thou art gone; and this fair island, wall'd
With the impregnable, unmaster'd sea,
Mourns with a widow's grief for loss of thee,—
Should we repine, as if thou wert install'd
In Heaven too soon? Nay, I will shed no tear.
Thy work is done. It was enough for thee
To own the glorious might of Liberty,
And cast away the bondage and the fear
Of rotten custom; so the hope, which Fate
Snatch'd from thy life, thy Fame shall consumate.

The Dandelion

Strange plants we bring from lands where Caffirs roam,
And great the traveller in botanic fame
That can inflict his queer and ugly name
On product of South Afric sands or loam,
Or on the flexile creeper that hath clomb
Up the tall stems of Polynesian palms;
And now with clusters, or with spikes, embalms
The sickly air beneath the glassy dome
In lordly garden. Haply time may be
When botanist from fire-born Owhyhee
Shall bear thee, milky mother of white down,
Back to his isle, a golden gift superb; —
Give name uncouth to diuretic herb,
And from the Dandelion reap renown.

Prometheus

SCENE.—*A desolate spot, supposed to lie beyond the limits of the habitable earth.* PROMETHEUS *discovered chained to a rock. Soft Music is heard in the distance, which, as it gradually draws nearer, becomes graver and slower.*

Chorus of SYLPHS *on the wing, who enter singing as follows:—*

Lightly tripping o'er the land,
Deftly skimming o'er the main,
Scarce our fairy wings bedewing
With the frothy mantling brine,
Scarce our silver feet acquainting
With the verdure-vested ground;
Now like swallows o'er a river
Gliding low with quivering pinion,
Now aloft in ether sailing
Leisurely as summer cloud;
Rising now, anon descending,
Swift and bright as shooting stars,
Thus we travel glad and free.

Deep in a wilderness of bloom,
We felt the shaking of the air
Blown o'er deserts vast and idle,
O'er ambrosial fields of flowers,
O'er many a league, where never man
Imprest his footstep o'er the sand,

Or shook the dry and husky seeds
From the tall and feathery grass.

But 'twas not the liquid voice
Of warbling Nymphs their sea-love soothing,
'Twas not the billows of the breeze
That tells when sister Sylphs are coming;
Nay, 'twas a sound of terror and woe,
A noise of force and striving:
It was not the meeting of icebergs,
Whose crash might out-thunder the thunderer,
And their glare make the lightning look dim;
It was not the storm of the secret ocean,
That lashes the shore to the wild bear's howling;
For the loud-throated tempests are silent with horror,
And the sea stands still in amaze.
'Twas the piercing cry of immortal agony,
That taught a strange tongue to the first unkind echoes
Of this dull lump of earth, this joyless mountain.

[*Perceiving* PROMETHEUS]

Oh, sight of fear!
What shape is that, what goodly form divine,
That in yon bare and storm-beleaguer'd rift
Stands like a mark for sun and frosty wind
By turns to waste their idle shafts upon?
How horribly it glares! No sign of life,
Save in the ghastly rolling of those eyes!
Lives it, indeed? Or is the loathing spirit
Pent in a corse, a gaol, a hulk of flesh,
That is no more its own? Oh! do not look at it,
Or we shall all grow like it. Let us hence,—

Yet, hold! it breathes; methinks that I should know—
Hark! did he stir? Oh, no, he cannot!—fast,
Fast as a frozen sea, quite motionless!
Though every sinew stares as he were bent
To unfix the mountain from its rooted base,
And whelm us with the ruins! Ah, poor wretch!
The mountain shall as soon unfix itself
As he wipe off the sweat-drop from his brow,
Or make his bosom lighter by a sigh,
He is so fast impaled. His noble limbs
And spacious bulk, as tightly manacled
As a fair gazelle in the serpent's coil,
And every feature of his face grown stiff
With the hard look of agony.

    PROMETHEUS.   Oh, me!

    SYLPH. Behold, his teeth unlock, his black lips ope,
As he would speak to us! Oh, thou sad spectacle!

    PROMETHEUS. What now? Is aught forgotten?
Hath the God,
With his wise council, hatch'd some new device
To plague the rebel? Is it not enough?
Nay, be not slack; ye're welcome:—sweet were a change,
If but a change of tortures! But to grow
A motionless rock, fast as my strong prison,
Age after age, till circling suns outnumber
The sands upon the tide-worn beach. No hope,
Or that sad mockery of hope that fools
With dull despair, spanning the infinite!
Torment unmeasurable!

    SYLPH.   Alas! art thou
The lofty-soul'd Prometheus?

PROMETHEUS.   Ay! the fool
That dared the wrath of Jove, hated of all
That share his feasts and crouch before his throne;
The mighty seer, the wise Prometheus.
Ah, for himself not wise! Poor, poor weak slaves,
Do ye not scorn me? But I cannot shake,
Or ye might see how fearful I am grown,
That nought have more to fear!

SYLPH.   Oh, fear not us!
A long, long way we come to visit thee;
    To this extreme of earth
    On clipping pinions borne.

    For the grating of fetters,
    The voice of upbraiding,
    The deep, earthly groan
    Of anguish half-stifled;
    The ear-piercing shriek
    Of pain in its sharpness, —

A concert, all tuneless, came ruffling the rose-buds,
Where sweetly we slumber'd the sultry hours;
So with pinions unsmooth'd, and tresses unbraided,
Our bright feet unsandall'd, we leap'd on the air.
Like the sound of the trumpet we shook the wide ether.
A moment we quiver'd, then glancing on high,
Ascended a sun-ray, light pillar of silver,
And seem'd the gay spangles that danced in the beam.
Soon in the cool and clear expanse
Of upper air we sail'd, so fleet, so smooth,
Our feathery oars we waved not, and that flight,

Which left whole empires in its rear uncounted,
As bubbles in the wake of some swift bark,
Seem'd like a sleep of endless blessedness.
Thus floating, we arrived
At the last confines of the fair creation;
Right o'er this spot unholy,
Where tired Nature left her work half done.
Oh, how unlike those happy fields of light
Where late we voyaged! The thick, dark air,
Still pressing earthward, closes o'er our heads
With dull and leaden sound, like sleepy waters.

PROMETHEUS. Never till this day
Did life disturb the dense eternity
Of joyless quiet; never skylark's song,
Or storm-bird's prescient scream, or eaglet's cry,
Made vital the gross fog. The very light
Is but an alien that can find no welcome;
So horrible the silent solitude,
That e'en those vile artificers of wrong,
Brute instruments of ghastly cruelty,
Whose grisly faces were too fell to dream of,—
Even they seem'd comfortable when they turn'd
Their backs upon me! Oh, too bitter shame,
I could have wept to beg them tarry longer!

SYLPH. And didst thou weep? And did they leave thee thus?
Oh, pitiless slaves!

PROMETHEUS. No, I did not weep.
Fall'n as I am, I closed my eyelids hard;
They burn'd like fire, and seem'd as they were full.
But, no! the dew of tears was scorch'd away.
I did not—sure they could not see me—weep.

I bade them farewell, and my voice was firm:
I think it made them tremble, for the sound
Of their departure seem'd to shun my ear,
As they had done some perilous deed in haste,
And dared not look on it. They stole away:
The patter of their feet still fretted me,
Like drops in caves that evermore are ceasing,
Yet never cease, so long they seem'd agoing.
Methought 'twere joy to heave a groan unheard,
Unmark'd of coward scorn. Nay, do not weep,
Or I shall e'en heap shame upon my shame,
And all that remains of god in me
Be quench'd in tears. Alas, my gentle sprights!
But now I wish to glide into a stream,
And lose myself in ocean's liberty,
Leaving my empty chains a monument
And hollow trophy of the tyrant's rage;
Or be a lump of ice which you might thaw
With the kind warmth of sighs. And hard I strove
To put away my immortality,
Till my collected spirits swell'd my heart
Almost to bursting; but the strife is past.
It is a fearful thing to be a god,
And, like a god, endure a mortal's pain;
To be a show for earth and wondering heaven
To gaze and shudder at! But I will live,
That Jove may know there is a deathless soul
Who ne'er will be his subject. Yes, 'tis past.
The stedfast Fates confess my absolute will,—
Their own co-equal. I have struggled long,
And single-handed, with their triple power,

And most opposing, still been most their slave.
And yet, the will survived: Lord of itself;
Free to disclaim the forseen forced effect
Of its free workings. Now, we are agreed,
I and my destinies. The total world,—
Above, below, whate'er is seen or known,
And all that men, and all that gods enact,
Hopes, fears, imaginations, purposes;
With joy, and pain, and every pulse that beats
In the great body of the universe,
I give to the eternal sisterhood,
To make my peace withal! And cast this husk,
This hated, mangled, and dishonour'd carcase
Into the balance; so have I redeem'd
My power, birthright, even the changeless mind,
The imperishable essence uncontroll'd.

    SYLPH. Strange talk, Prometheus! Every scornful word,
And every bitter boast, may add an age
Of torture to thy doom. We would in truth
That we might melt thy fetters with our sighs!
But what we can, we will. Hold but thy peace;
Or, if thou wilt forbid us, scoff, revile,
But let us beg for thee. Our wilful prayer,
By thee forbidden, leaves thy pride unstain'd,
Thy will unmaster'd. He did love us once:
The mighty Jove did love us. Did? He does.
There is a spell of unresisted power
In wonder-working weak simplicity,
Because it is not fear'd.

    PROMETHEUS.   Fair creature, pause!
I am not so ungentle as to chide

The idle chirpings of imprison'd love,
That warbles freely in its narrow cage;
But I would bid the nightingale be dumb,
Or ere her amorous descant should betray
Her covert to the spoiler.

    SYLPH.   Spare thy fears;
For we have winning wiles and sorceries,
Such incantations as thy sterner wit
Did never dream of. Time hath been ere now
That Jove hath listen'd to our minstrelsy,
Till wrath would seem to drop out of his soul
Like a forgotten thing. Our smallest note,
Catching his ear at any breathing space
Amid his loudest threats, would make him mute
As wondering childhood. True, the fault is great,
But we are many that will plead for thee;
We and our sisters, dwellers in the streams
That murmur blithely to the joyous mood,
And dolefully to sadness. Not a nook
In darkest woods but some of us are there,
To watch the flowers, that else would die unseen.
And some there are that live among the wells
Of hidden waters in the central earth,
Or keep their state in caves where diamonds grow.
And the soft amethyst and emerald
Bask in the streamy and perpetual light
Of that mysterious stone that owes the day
No tribute for its lustre: in whose beam
A thousand gems give out their thousand hues,
As to their proper sun; not, as on earth,
By art and toil enforced. Our sisters, they,

The friendly sprites, to thee, I guess, well known,
Who show the swains where treasured fountains lie;
And those who used to guide thee in thy quest
For the earth's riches, brass and valued gold.

  PROMETHEUS. I well remember, for I know you all,
Where'er ye sojourn, and whatever names
Ye are or shall be called; fairies, or sylphs,
Nymphs of the wood or mountain, flood or field:
Live ye in peace, and long may ye be free
To follow your good minds.

  SYLPH.   Ah, that we will!
Are we not bold to bid a god repent;
To break upon his slumbers with our prayers;
To watch him day and night; to wear him out
With endless supplication? Perhaps to beg
His kind attention to a pleasant tale;
To cheat him into pity, and conclude
Each story with Prometheus?

  PROMETHEUS.   Bold and rash!

  SYLPH. He shall not 'scape us. Not a hold secure
In all his empire but our airy host
Shall there prevent him. If in quaint disguise
He roam the earth, or float adown the streams
To tempt or Naiad's love, or woman's eye,
Though watchful Juno were deceived, yet we
Should know him still. Ha! then should be our time.
Surprise him then, there's nought he can refuse,
Lest we expose him to the laughing sky,
As Vulcan did the War-god. Yet no shape
Of dreadful majesty, nor sacred haunt,
Our close and passionate suit shall overawe;

For he shall hear us in the vocal gloom
Of green Dodona's leafy wilderness,
And where from all apart he oft retires
To brood upon his glory. Ours shall be
The one request that he shall ever hear
Till thou are pardon'd. Can he then be stern,
When all the praise, the sweetness of his reign,
The joy that he was glad to look upon,
The boundless ether's fitful harmony,
And the wild music of the ocean caves,
Is turn'd to sighing and importunate grief
For poor Prometheus?

    PROMETHEUS.   Gentle powers, forbear!
'Twere worse than all my former miseries
Should my huge wreck suck down the friendly skiff
That proffer'd aidance. Oh! that Jupiter
Had hurl'd me to the deep of Erebus,
Where neither god nor man might pity me.
Where I might be unthought of as the star
Last outpost of the bright celestial band,
That walks its circuit of a thousand years,
Shooting faint rays at black infinity.
But now shall I become a common tale,
A ruin'd fragment of a worn-out world;
Unchanging record of unceasing change,
Eternal landmark to the tide of time.
Swift generations, that forget each other,
Shall still keep up the memory of my shame
Till I am grown an unbelieved fable.
Horsed upon hippogriffs, the hags of night
Shall come to visit me; and once an age

Some desperate wight, or wizard, gaunt and grey,
Shall seek this spot by help of hidden lore,
To ask of things forgotten or to come.
But who, beholding me, shall dare defy
The wrath of Jove? Since vain is wisdom's boast,
And impotent the knowledge that o'erleaps
The dusky bourne of time. 'Twere better far
That gods should quaff their nectar merrily,
And men sing out the day like grasshoppers,
So may they haply lull the watchful thunder.

    SYLPH. Ah, happy men, whose evil destiny,
Self-baffled, falls! The fellest storm that blows,
The soonest wafts them to an endless calm.
Would we were mortal!

    PROMETHEUS.   Wherefore would ye so?
What coy delight awakes to sun or stars
But e'en a thought conveys you to the cradle
Of its young sweetness?

    SYLPH.   True; but what delight
Shall dare awake while all the spacious world
Is anguish with the terror of thy pains,
And sick for thy affliction?

    PROMETHEUS.   You, at least,
Have nought to fear. Your unsubstantial forms
Present no scope to the keen thunderbolt;
Nor adamant can bind your subtle essence,
Which is as fine as scent of violets,
Quick as the warbled notes of melody,
And unconfinable as thoughts of gods.
Then go your way. Forget Prometheus,
And all the woe that he is doom'd to bear;

By his own choice this vile estate preferring
To ignorant bliss and unfelt slavery.

    SYLPH. Well, we will go, but never to forget
Thee, nor omit thy cause. 'Tis vain to strive,
For Jove is not one half so merciless
As thou art to thyself. But fare thee well;
Our love is all as stubborn as thy pride,
And swift as firm. For ere yon full-orb'd moon,
That now emerges from that dark confine,
And, scaling slow the steep opposed heaven,
Is red and swoln, assume her silvery veil
And high career of virgin quietness,
Shall we alight upon the topmost peak
Of Jove's Olympus.

    PROMETHEUS. Ye are free to go
Where'er ye will, but not to plead for him
Whom Jove abhors. No, not to pity him,
Or ye may wish your errant range of wing
Were narrow as the evening beetle's rounds.

    SYLPH. Not free to pity! What were Jove himself
If pity had not been? Was he not once
A hapless babe, condemn'd to die ere born?
But when he smiled, unweeting of his doom,
And press'd his little hand on Rhea's bosom,
Then gentle pity touch'd his mother's heart,
Till very softness made her bold to brave
The sternness of her hoary husband's ire.
Oh, we have hung upon our motionless wings,
And watch'd her bending sadly o'er his cradle,
Shading his rosy face with her dark locks
In such sweet stillness of o'ermaster'd sorrow,

As if she fear'd a sigh might wake her bird,
Or call his ruthless father to devour him.
And when at length e'en love to love gave way,
And she consented to resign the babe,
To the kind nymph who promised to conceal him,
With all a mother's tender fortitude,
She wash'd the tear-drops from his fair round cheeks
With rain from her own eyes; for she was melted,
Yet nothing shaken. Pity made her firm.
Yet when the Oread virgin turn'd away,
And he, with baby cries, stretch'd out his arms
Over her ivory shoulders, well I ween
She would have given her godhead for a heart
That might have broken. Then we sang our songs,
And soothed her melancholy thoughts with tales
How he should come to be a mighty god,
And blast his foes with fiery thunderbolts.
And day by day, in sunshine or in storm,
We posted 'twixt far Ida and Olympus
To bear her kisses to her growing babe,
And bring back daily tidings of his weal.
He was a lovely child, a boy divine;
And joy'd to listen to the gurgling music
of Ida's many streams. We little thought
That he would prove so stern and tyrannous.

    PROMETHEUS. 'Tis ever so. Full many an innocent flower
Is womb and cradle to a poisonous berry.
Mark the cub lion, stolen from its dam,
Loved playmate of the youngling foresters,
Who laugh to see it shake its maneless neck,
And lash with little tail, and beat the earth

In angry sportiveness. Wait but awhile,
That lion's roar, like the low thunder-groan,
That rumbles under foot before an earthquake,
Shall send a horrible silence o'er the waste,
That every living thing shall send away,
Like shadow'd clouds when sun and moon are striving.

SYLPH. And yet 'twas sweet to listen to his tales,
And watch the strivings of the god within him.
For all his prattle and his childishness
Were godlike, full of hope and prophecy.
And so he waxëd lusty, fair, and tall,
And added sinew changed his baby flesh,
That dimpled erst at every touch of love;
And the loose ringlets of his silky hair
Knotted in crisper curls. His deepening voice
Told like a cavern'd oracle the fall
Of sky-throned dynasties. He grew, and grew,
A star-bright sign of fated empery;
And all conspiring omens led him on
To lofty purpose and pre-eminence.
The mountain eagles, towering in their pride,
Stoop'd at his beck and flock'd about his path,
Like the small birds by wintry famine tamed;
Or with their dusky and expansive wings
Shaded and fann'd him as he slept at noon.
The lightnings danced before him sportively,
And shone innocuous as the pale cold moon
In the clear blue of his celestial eye.
Oft the nigh thunder-clap, o'er Ida's peak,
Chiding the echoes that bemock'd it, paused,
And with a low abasëd voice did homage

To its predestined Lord. But more than all,
With no ambiguous sign, the gifted Themis,
Thy mother, O Prometheus! pointed out
The very spot—a lovely spot it was,
Untrodden then, and wild, without a sound,
Save old Æsopus and his lovely song,
Where the glad sons of the deliver'd earth
Shall yearly raise their multitudinous voice,
Hymning great Jove, the God of Liberty!
Then he grew proud, yet gentle in his pride,
And full of tears, which well became his youth,
As showers do spring. For he was quickly moved,
And joy'd to hear sad stories that we told
Of what we saw on earth, of death and woe,
And all the waste of time. Then would he swear
That he would conquer time; that in his reign
It never should be winter; he would have
No pain, no growing old, no death at all.
And that the pretty damsels, whom we said
He must not love, for they would die and leave him,
Should evermore be young and beautiful;
Or, if they must go, they should come again,
Like as the flowers did. Thus he used to prate,
Till we almost believed him. Oft at eve
We sang the glories of the coming age,
And oft surprised the wanderer in the woods
With bodements sweet of immortality.

    PROMETHEUS. Aye, ye wert blest with folly. Who may tell
What strange conceits upon the earth were sown
And gender'd by the fond garrulity
Of your aëreal music? Scatter'd notes,

Half heard, half fancied by the erring sense
Of man, on which they fell like downy seeds
Sown by autumnal winds, grew up, and teem'd
With plenteous madness. Legends marvellous
Of golden ages past, and dreams as wild,
As sweetly wild, of that auspicious birth,
That glorious advent of delight unfading,
Which brooks, and vesper gales, and all divine
Mysterious melodies, in sleep or trance,
Or lonely musing heard, to that blind race
So oft announced. Vain phantasies and hopes,
That shall be hopes for aye, from sire to son
Descending; chaunted in a hundred tongues
By errant minstrels borne from land to land,
And in the storm-bewilder'd bark convey'd
To furthest isles, where yet unheard of man
The surges roar around. The various tribes,
Condemn'd alike to ever-present woe,
With various phantoms of futurity
Shall soothe their weary hour. Beneath the wain
of slow Bootes, where a mimic moon,
Like fiery ensign of a spiritual host,
Flick'ring and rustling, streams along the sky;
Where the black pine-woods splinter in the blast
That rides tempestuous o'er a wilderness
Of ancient snow, whose ineffectual gleam
Thwarts the pale darkness of the long long night
And Ocean, slumbering in his icy bed,
Hears not the shrill alarum of the storm.
There Scalds uncouth, in horrid accents screaming,
To clash of arms and outcries terrible,

Tuning their song, shall tell of shadowy realms
Where the brave dead, the mighty of old time,
Urge the fierce hunt, the bloody banquet share,
And drink deep draught nectareous from the skulls
Of slaughter'd foes. But in the perfumed groves,
Of the soft, languid, dreaming Orient,
And where, 'mid billowy sands, in the broad eye
Of an unprofitable, dewless heaven,
The lonely phœnix roams, shall hoary seers
And pensive shepherds, to believing maids
And meekest mothers, when their babes are hush'd,
Repeat the cherish'd tale at eventide,
Of a new world where peace shall ever dwell.
No armed hoof shall crush the daisy bold
That flaunts it in the sun, nor ambush'd foe
Invade the lurking violet in her bower,
Where beauty fades not, love is ever true,
And life immortal like a summer day.
Oh! happy creatures that, uncursed with love,
Look for a land they know not where, but deem
It may be girdled by the burning waste,
Or safely treasured in the secret ocean;
Or, haply, in the moon, where they shall live
Beneath the sole and everlasting sway
Of him, the babe benign, mighty and wise,
Whose might and wisdom are but innocence
And childish simpleness. Thrice happy they
Who ne'er have found and never can believe
That innocence is mere defect of might—
Simplicity the very craft of Nature,
To hide the piteous void of ignorance,

Till guile is grown of age. Too soon 'tis seen
The great are ever best when least themselves.
The weakest wind that wantons with your curls,
Grown strong would be a scouring hurricane.

    SYLPH. Alas! thy words are like this spot, unholy.
Thou could'st not speak them in a better place.

    PROMETHEUS. What place so holy where they are not true?
Ye see no tumult in the host of stars,
No taint of falsehood in the clear blue sky.
Yet there was ancient Uranus enthroned
And treason impious, foul, unnatural,
O'erwhelm'd his stellar and primeval seat
With horror and with shame.

    SYLPH.   And pleasant hills were those
Where the vast brood of Titan used to dwell,
Bathing their golden locks in morning light,
And sunn'd with even's latest, sweetest smile —
Her parting smile that bids the earth adieu.
Where are they gone, that giant brotherhood,
Lords of the mountains?

                      Past like clouds away,
And seen no more — save when their misty shades,
Among the lonely peaks they loved so well,
Far off beheld, astound the mountaineer.

    PROMETHEUS. Ay, they are gone; and he that holds their
       place
Is like them, strong and blind. What wonder, then,
Though he fall mightily?

    SYLPH.   The tale is told
Of Uranus and old Hyperion,
And that great mother: huge and sluggish powers

That just awoke from their eternal sleep
To gaze upon the new and vacant world,
Then sank to sleep again. And glad were we
When Saturn and his howling train were sent
To fright their slumbers in the nether void.
But must the youthful thunder-wielder fall,
For whom we sung the song of victory?
Fall from his high, his unapproached throne,
Which never god may touch, nor mortal eye
Pierce through the veil of congregated clouds,
That wave on wave, a dark and soundless sea,
Beneath it ebb and flow? Thus islanded,
It hangs enshrined in clear and crystal air,
And owns no kindred with the lower orb.
Oft we have seen that solitary height,
As gay we glanced athwart the sunny beam,
Or wash'd our pinions in the unfall'n dew,
And thought no peril and no change were there.

    PROMETHEUS. 'Tis a fair spot, and holy. I have known
When Rhea's boy hath wonder'd what it was,
That other silver star that staid behind,
When Phosphor left the sky. Yet now he deems
His godhead as the light immutable,
That cares not whether it be morn or even.

    SYLPH. There is a dark foreboding in thy speech;
Thine eyes flash fearfully a moody joy
That argues a new downfall. Whence arise
These desperate hopes, that seem to make thee fond
Of lowest misery?

    PROMETHEUS. I know it all—
All ye would ask. But ne'er shall hope be mine

Till the dread secret works its fatal will
In daylight visible, with wrath and scorn,
And ceaseless memory of forgotten things.
Then Jove shall learn what all his sulphurous bolts,
Soul-piercing torments, earthquakes, fiery plagues,
Disease, and hateful, black deformity,
And all confounding shame, shall ne'er persuade
My voice to utter.

CONCLUSION

Ye patient fields, rejoice!
The blessing that ye pray for silently
Is come at last; for ye shall no more fade,
Nor see your flow'rets droop like famishing babes
Upon your comfortless breasts. Close, pent-up woods!
Open your secrets to the prying sun;
For den nor forest dark shall longer hide
The noisome thing. Take heart, poor flutterer!
Nor fear the glitter of the serpent's eye:
No more it shines to harm thee. Sing aloud,
Toss high the shrillness of thy gurgling throat,
And wake the silence of Olympian bowers,
That Jove may hear thee—he, the lovely boy,
The son of Saturn, mightier than his sire,
And gentler far. Thou hollow earth! resound,
And, like the maddening drum of Cybele,
Roll with delight thro' all the sparry caves
A many-echoed peal. And, oh! ye soft
And wandering elements—ye sighing floods—

And thou, great treasury of light and music—
Embracing air with all your wealth of sounds,
And bodiless hues, and shadows glorified,
Of what on earth is terrible and fair
The fairer effluence and the living form,
With all your music, loud and lustily,
With every dainty joy of sight and smell,
Prepare a banquet meet to entertain
The Lord of Thunder, that hath set you free
From old oppression. Melancholy brook!
That creep'st along so dull and drowsily,
Wailing and waiting in the lazy noon,
In merry madness roar, and whirl, and bound,
Blithe as thy mountain sisters. Ne'er again
Shall summer drought, or icy manacle,
Obstruct thy tuneful liberty. Thou breeze,
That mak'st and organ of the mighty sea,
Obedient to thy wilful phantasies,
Provoke him not to scorn; but soft and low,
As pious maid awakes her aged sire,
On tiptoe stealing, whisper in his ear
The tidings of the young god's victory.
Then shall he rouse him on his rocky bed,
And join the universal hymn with strains
Of solemn thankfulness and deep delight—
The blended sweetness of a thousand waves.
But where is he, the voice intelligent
Of Nature's minstrelsy? Oh, where is man—
That mortal god, that hath no mortal kin
Or like on earth? Shall Nature's orator—
The interpreter of all her mystic strains—

Shall he be mute in Nature's jubilee?
Wilt thou be last in bliss and benison
That wast the first in lamentable wail,
And sole in conscious pain? Haply he fears
The bitter doom, that out of sweetness makes
Its sad memorial. Mortal! Fear no more,—
The reign is past of ancient violence;
And Jove hath sworn that time shall not deface,
Nor death destroy, nor mutability
Perplex the truth of love.

Song

Say—what is worse than blank despair,
'Tis that sick hope too weak for flying,
That plays at fast and loose with care,
And wastes a weary life in dying.

Though promise be a welcome guest,
Yet may it be too late a comer,
'Tis but a cuckoo voice at best,
The joy of spring, scarce heard in summer.

Then now consent, this very hour,
Let the kind word of peace be spoken;
Like dew upon a withered flower,
Is comfort to the heart that's broken.

The heart, whose will is from above,
Shall yet its mortal taint discover,
For Time, that cannot alter love,
Has power to slay the wretched lover.

Spenser

Sweet was the youth of virgin Poesy,
That virgin sweetness which she gave to thee,
My SPENSER, bard of happy innocence!
For thou didst with a bridegroom's love intense
Caress the fair inventions of thy brain,
Those babes of paradise, without the pain
Of mortal birth, to fairest heritage
Born in the freshness of their perfect age.
Thy Faery Knight had all the world in fee,
For all the world was Faeryland to thee.
Thine is no tale, once acted, then forgot;
Thy creatures never were, and never will be not.
Oh! look not for them in the dark abyss
Where all things have been, and where nothing is—
The spectral past;—nor in the troubled sea
Where all strange fancies are about to be—
The unabiding present. Seek them where
For ever lives the Good, the True, the Fair,
In the eternal silence of the heart.
There Spenser found them; thence his magic art
Their shades evoked in feature, form, and limb,
Real as a human self, and bright as cherubim.
And what though wistful love and emulous arms,
And all the wizard might of mutter'd charms,—
Though slimy snakes disgorge their loathly rage,
And monstrous phantoms wait on Archimage:

These are but dreams, that come, and go, and peep
Through the thin curtain of a morning sleep,
And leave no pressure on the soul, that wakes
And hails the glad creation that it makes.

Donne

Brief was the reign of pure poetic truth;
A race of thinkers next, with rhymes uncouth,
And fancies fashion'd in laborious brains,
Made verses heavy as o'erloaded wains.
Love was their theme, but love that dwelt in stones,
Or charm'd the stars in their concentric zones;
Love that did first the nuptial bond conclude
'Twixt immaterial form and matter rude;
Love that was riddled, sphered, transacted, spelt,
Sublimed, projected, everything but felt.
Or if in age, in orders, or the cholic,
They damn'd all loving as a heathen frolic;
They changed their topic, but in style the same,
Adored their Maker as they would their dame.
Thus DONNE, not first, but greatest of the line,
Of stubborn thoughts a garland thought to twine;
To his fair maid brought cabalistic posies,
And sung quaint ditties of metempsychosis;
Twists iron pokers into true love-knots,
Coining hard words, not found in polyglots.

Lines

Oh for a man, I care not what he be,
A lord or a labourer, so his soul be free,
Who had one spark of that celestial fire
That did the Prophets of old time inspire,
When Joel made the mystic trumpet cry,
When Jeremiah raised his voice on high,
And rapt Isaiah felt his great heart swell
With all the sins and woes of Israel!
Not such am I,—a petty man of rhyme,
Nursed in the softness of a female time.
From May of life to Autumn have I trod
The earth, not quite unconscious of my God;
But apter far to recognise his power
In sweet perfection of a pencill'd flower,
A kitten's gambols, or a birdie's nest,
A baby sleeping on its mother's breast,
Than in the fearful passages of life,—
That battle-field, the never-ceasing strife
Of policy that ever would be wise,
Dissecting truth into convenient lies;
The gallows, or the press-gang, or the press;
The poor man's pittance, ever less and less;
The dread magnificence of ancient crime,
Or the mean mischief of the present time.
Yet there is something in my heart that would
Become a witness to eternal good.
Woe to the man that wastes his wealth of mind,
And leaves no legacy to human kind!

I love my country well,—I love the hills,
I love the valleys and the vocal rills;
But most I love the men, the maids, the wives,
The myriad multitude of human lives.

To a Cat

Nelly, methinks, 'twixt thee and me,
There is a kind of sympathy;
And could we interchange our nature,—
If I were cat, thou human creature,—
I should, like thee, be no great mouser,
And thou, like me, no great composer;
For, like thy plaintive mews, my muse,
With villainous whine doth fate abuse,
Because it has not made me sleek
As golden down on Cupid's cheek;
And yet thou canst upon the rug lie,
Stretch'd out like snail, or curl'd up snugly,
As if thou wert not lean or ugly;
And I, who in poetic flights
Sometimes complain of sleepless nights
Regardless of the sun in heaven,
Am apt to dose till past eleven.
The world would just the same go round
If I were hang'd and thou wert drown'd;
There is one difference, 'tis true,—
Thou dost not know it, and I do.

Stay Where Thou Art

Stay where thou art, thou canst not better be,
For thou art pure and noble as thou'rt sweet,
And thy firm faith still working, will complete
A lovely picture of the Deity.
For 'tis in thee, mild maid, and such as thee,
Whose goodness would make any features fair,
I find the hope that bids me not despair,
But know there is a Saviour even for me.
May God in mercy from thy knowledge hide
All but the path in which thou art advancing.
For evil things there are, on either side,
Dark flames on one, like antic demons dancing,
And on the left a desert waste and wide,
Where is no chart, no compass, and no guide.

Prayer

There is an awful quiet in the air,
And the sad earth, with moist imploring eye,
Looks wide and wakeful at the pondering sky,
Like Patience slow subsiding to Despair.
But see, the blue smoke as a voiceless prayer,
Sole witness of a secret sacrifice,
Unfolds its tardy wreaths, and multiplies
Its soft chameleon breathings in the rare
Capacious ether,—so it fades away,
And nought is seen beneath the pendant blue,
The undistinguishable waste of day.
So have I dream'd!—oh, may the dream be true!—
That praying souls are purged from mortal hue,
And grow as pure as He to whom they pray.

Could I But Harmonise . . .

Could I but harmonise one kindly thought,
Fix one fair image in a snatch of song,
Which maids might warble as they tripped along;
Or could I ease the labouring heart, o'erfraught
With passionate truths for which the mind untaught
Lacks form or utterance, with a single line;
Might rustic lovers woo in phrase of mine,
I should not deem that I have lived for nought;
The world were welcome to forget my name,
Could I bequeath a few remembered words
Like his, the bard who never dreamed of fame,
Whose rhymes preserve from harm the pious birds;
Or his, that dim full many a star-bright eye
With woe for Barbara Allen's cruelty.

Moses in the Bulrushes

She left her babe, and went away to weep,
And listen'd oft to hear if he did cry;
But the great river sung his lullaby,
And unseen angels fann'd his balmy sleep.
And yet his innocence itself might keep;
The sacred silence of his slumb'rous smile
Makes peace in all the monster-breeding Nile;
For God e'en now is moving in the sweep
Of mighty waters. Little dreams the maid,
The royal maid, that comes to woo the wave
With her smooth limbs beneath the trembling shade
Of silver-chaliced lotus, what a child
Her freak of pity is ordain'd to save!
How terrible the thing that looks so mild!

Faith—How Guarded

Yes, thou dost well, to arm thy tender mind
With all that learning, and stern common sense
Living hath spoke, or dying left behind;
To blank the frowardness of pert pretence
With long experience of a mighty mind,
That, daring to explore the truth immense,
Subsided in a faithful reverence
Of the best Catholic hope of human kind.
Yes, thou dost well to build a fence about
Thine inward faith, and mount a stalwart guard
Of answers, to oppose invading doubt.
All aids are needful, for the strife is hard;
But still be sure the truth within to cherish,—
Truths long besieged too oft of hunger perish.

'Twere Surely Hard . . .

'Twere surely hard to toil without an aim.
Then shall the toil of an immortal mind
Spending its strength for good of human kind
Have no reward on earth but empty fame?
Oh, say not so. 'Tis not the echoed name,
Dear though it be—dear to the wafting wind,
That is not all the poet leaves behind,
That once has kindled an undying flame.
And what is that? It is a happy feeling
Begot by bird, or flower, or vernal bee.
'Tis aught that acts, unconsciously revealing
To mortal man his immortality.
Then think, O Poet, think how bland, how healing,
The beauty thou hast taught thy fellow man to see.

Night

The crackling embers on the hearth are dead;
The indoor note of industry is still;
The latch is fast; upon the window sill
The small birds wait not for their daily bread;
The voiceless flowers—how quietly they shed
Their nightly odours;—and the household rill,
Murmurs continuous dulcet sounds that fill
The vacant expectation, and the dread
Of listening night. And haply now she sleeps;
For all the garrulous noises of the air
Are hush'd in peace; the soft dew silent weeps,
Like hopeless lovers for a maid so fair—
Oh! that I were the happy dream that creeps
To her soft heart, to find my image there.

'Multum Dilexit'

She sat and wept beside His feet; the weight
Of sin oppress'd her heart; for all the blame,
And the poor malice of the worldly shame,
To her was past, extinct, and out of date,
Only the *sin* remain'd,—the leprous state;
She would be melted by the heat of love,
By fires far fiercer than are blown to prove
And purge the silver ore adulterate.
She sat and wept, and with her untress'd hair
Still wiped the feet she was so blest to touch;
And He wiped off the soiling of despair
From her sweet soul, because she loved so much.
I am a sinner, full of doubts and fears,
Make me a humble thing of love and tears.

1848

Biographical Sketch[1]

'The outward events of our dear Hartley's life', wrote Sara
Coleridge, shortly after her brother's death from bronchitis on 6
January 1849, 'are few and slight . . . There is little to tell, but
much to describe . . .'[2] Hartley Coleridge's life was not an event-
ful one. He spent his childhood running free around Keswick,
and his school years under the aegis of an indulgent master. After
studying at Merton College Oxford, he failed his probationary
year as a fellow at Oriel and then spent a couple of years trying
to earn a living as a writer in London, before his father forced
him to return to the Lake District to work as a teacher. During
the 1830s, he lived in Leeds for two years, writing biographies
for a publisher who eventually went bankrupt, and then returned
to the Lakes, spending the rest of his life writing, talking, drinking
and wandering, supported financially by his family, and adored
by the locals. He never married, but often fell in love. It's not
known if these infatuations were ever reciprocal, as, apparently,
he never dared to act on his feelings, believing himself too ugly,
odd and poor to attract women.[3]

---

1. Despite the competent and well-researched biography written by Earl Leslie
   Griggs: *Hartley Coleridge: His Life and Work* (University of London Press,
   1929), the best account of Hartley's life is still to be found in the memoir
   written by his brother Derwent, which prefixes the 1851 edition of Hartley's
   poetry.
2. S. Coleridge, *Memoir and Letters of Sara Coleridge, Edited by her Daughter*,
   vol.II, p.217.
3. 'Without being an ugly fellow,' wrote Southey to John Taylor, 'he is a
   marvellously odd one – he is very short, with remarkably strong features,
   some of the thickest and blackest eyebrows you ever saw, and a beard which
   a Turk might envy. His manners are as peculiar as his appearance, and
   having discovered that he is awkward by nature, he has formed an unhappy

Named after the philosopher David Hartley, who at that time Samuel Taylor Coleridge admired hugely (the David was dropped by the time of his christening), Hartley Coleridge was born on 19 September 1796, the first child of Samuel Taylor and Sarah Coleridge (née Fricker). The poet proved a besotted father, who as well as changing nappies, wrote exquisite verses about and for his son. His feelings and hopes for Hartley are best expressed in these lines from 'Frost at Midnight':

> My babe so beautiful! it thrills my heart
> With tender gladness, thus to look at thee,
> And think that thou shalt learn far other lore,
> And in far other scenes! For I was reared
> In the great city, pent 'mid cloisters dim,
> And saw nought lovely but the sky and stars.
>
> But *thou*, my babe! shalt wander like a breeze
> By lakes and sandy shores, beneath the crags
> Of ancient mountain, and beneath the clouds,
> Which image in their bulk both lakes and shores
> And lovely shapes and sounds intelligible
> Of that eternal language, which thy God
> Utters, who from eternity doth teach
> Himself in all, and all things in himself.
> Great universal Teacher! he shall mould
> Thy spirit, and by giving make it ask.

Hartley Coleridge did get to 'wander like a breeze / By lakes and sandy shores, beneath the crags / Of ancient mountain, and

---

conclusion that art will never make him otherwise, and so resigns himself to his fate . . .'

beneath the clouds'. In July 1800, the Coleridges moved from Nether Stowey near Bristol to Greta Hall, Keswick.

'Our house', STC wrote to his friend and brother-in-law Southey, 'stands on a low hill, the whole front of which is one field and an enormous garden, nineteen-twentieths of which is an enormous nursery-garden. Behind the house is an orchard, on a steep slope, at the foot of which flows the river Greta, which winds round and catches the evening light at the front of the house.'[4]

Here, Hartley's brother Derwent (aka 'Stumpy Canary' because of a bright yellow outfit he often wore as an infant) and sister Sara were born in September 1800 and December 1802 respectively. In 1803, the Southeys, who had recently lost a child, came up for a recuperative visit – and stayed for the rest of their lives. That September, STC, neither healthy nor happy, set off for London, and thence Malta; from then on was rarely at home, and Southey increasingly assumed responsibility for the Coleridge children. In 1802, Wordsworth wrote 'To H. C. six years old'. It provides a moving (in both senses of the word) picture of Hartley and is heavy with the poet's concerns for the boy's future.

> O thou! whose fancies from afar are brought;
> Who of thy words dost make a mock apparel,
> And fittest to unutterable thought
> The breeze-like motion and the self-born carol;
> Thou fairy voyager! that dost float
> In such clear water, that thy Boat
> May rather seem

4. D. Coleridge (ed.), *Poems by Hartley Coleridge*, p.xxiv, footnote.

To brood on air than on earthly stream;
Suspended in a stream as clear as sky,
Where earth and heaven do make one imagery;
O blessed Vision! happy child!
Thou art so exquisitely wild,
I think of thee with many fears
For what may be thy lot in future years,
I thought of times when Pain might be thy guest,
Lord of thy house and hospitality;
And Grief, uneasy lover! never rest,
But when she sat within the touch of thee.
O too industrious folly!
O vain and ceaseless melancholy!
Nature will either end thee quite;
Or, lengthening out thy season of delight,
Preserve for thee, by individual right,
A young lamb's heart among the full-grown flocks.
What hast thou to do with sorrow,
Or the injuries of to-morrow?
Thou art a Dew-drop, which morn brings forth,
Ill fitted to sustain unkindly shocks,
Or to be trailed along the soiling earth;
A gem that glitters while it lives,
And no forewarning gives;
But, at the touch of wrong, without a strife
Slips in a moment out of life.[5]

Hartley at six, then, was an 'exquisitely wild', glitteringly imagi-
native faery, living at one remove from reality, ill-equipped to

---

5. Ibid, p.xviii.

cope with grief or pain. He was also prone to temper tantrums, during which he would deliberately injure himself.

'His sensibility', wrote Derwent, 'was intense, and he had not the wherewithal to control it. He could not open a letter without trembling. He shrank from mental pain – he was beyond measure impatient of constraint. He was liable to paroxysms of rage, often the disguise of pity, self-accusation, or other painful emotion – anger it could hardly be called – during which he bit his arm or finger violently.'[6]

By the time he was eight, Hartley had found an outlet for his imagination: Ejuxria. Mrs Montagu[7] recalled this in a letter to Derwent:

> He had found a spot upon the globe which he peopled with an imaginary nation, gave them a name, a language, laws, and a senate; where he framed long speeches, which he translated, as he said, for my benefit, and for the benefit of my neighbours, who climbed the garden-wall to listen to this surprising child, whom they supposed to be reciting pieces from memory . . . He called this nation the 'Ejuxrii'; and one day, when walking very pensively, I asked him what ailed him. He said, 'My people are too fond of war, and I have just made an eloquent speech in the Senate, which has not made any impression on them, and to war they will go.'[8]

What seems unusual here is not Hartley's inventiveness – after all, lots of boys and girls create imaginary worlds of great

---

6. Ibid, p.lix.
7. With whom Hartley and his father stayed during Hartley's 1807 'annus mirabilis' trip to London, where he went to the theatre with Wordsworth, visited the Tower of London with Walter Scott, and learned chemistry from Humphrey Davy.
8. D. Coleridge (ed.), *Poems by Hartley Coleridge*, pp.xxxiii–xxxiv.

complexity – but, rather, the way in which the people and institutions of Ejuxria seem to exert power over *him* rather than vice versa. Most children, one might think, would succeed in persuading even thoroughly recalcitrant imaginary politicians to their point of view.

Derwent was Hartley's primary audience – 'the depository of all his thoughts and feelings, and in particular of that strange dream-life which . . . he led in the cloud-land of his fancy'.[9]

'His usual mode of introducing the subject was – "Derwent . . . I have had letters and papers from Ejuxria." Then came his budget of news, with appropriate reflections, his words flowing on in an exhaustless stream, and his countenance bearing witness to the inspiration . . . by which he was guided.'[10]

> Taken as a whole, the Ejuxrian world presented a complete analogon to the world of fact, so far as it was known to Hartley, complete in all its parts; furnishing a theatre and scene of action, with *dramatis personæ*, and suitable machinery, in which, day after day for the space of long years, he went on evolving the complicated drama of existence. There were many nations, continental and insular, each with its separate history, civil, ecclesiastical, and literary, its forms of religion and government and specific national character . . . The names of generals and statesmen were 'familiar to my ears as household words'. I witnessed the jar of faction, and had to trace the course of sedition. I lived to see changes of government, a great progress of public opinion, and a new order of things![11]

---

9. Ibid, p.xxxvi.
10. Ibid, p.xxxix.
11. Ibid, pp.xxxvii–xxxix.

Hartley never joined in the usual childhood games because, according to Derwent, he was 'incapable of the adroitness and presence of mind required in the most ordinary sports'. He describes how, after saving a child from drowning in the Greta, Hartley was given a bag of marbles by the child's grateful mother. 'She might as well have presented him with the balls of an Indian juggler for any use that he could make of them.'[12] He believed that his brother's rich imaginary life developed, to some extent, in compensation for these physical inadequacies – although it's just as plausible that the intricacies of the unreal simply proved overwhelmingly distracting. STC recorded Hartley, age seven, reproved for being unobservant, responding, 'I see it – I saw it, and to-morrow I shall see it again when I shut my eyes, and when my eyes are open, and I am looking at other things; but, father, it is a sad pity, but it cannot be helped, you know; but I am always being a bad boy when I am thinking of my thoughts.'[13]

Hartley and Derwent started school together in autumn 1808. The school was run by a great admirer of STC's who, much taken with Hartley's precocious eloquence, exerted little discipline over him. 'Mr. Dawes,' reported Derwent to his father, 'only *looks* at Hartley and never scolds *him*, and *all* the boys think it very unfair – he *is* a genius.' Being teacher's pet, as well as diminutive and strange, Hartley was teased mercilessly by older pupils. 'As a *little* boy,' recalled Derwent, 'he paid the usual penalty of helpless oddity. Though not persecuted with ... savagery ... he was *plagued* in a manner and to an extent of

---

12. Ibid, p.li.
13. S. Coleridge, *Memoir and Letters*, pp.4–5.

which . . . he never lost the impression.'[14] In his thirties Hartley wrote to his mother, describing the taunting and its long-term effects: 'When I am at all unwell . . . they [the older boys] are always at me in my dreams – hooting, pelting, spitting at me, stopping my ways, setting all sorts of hideous, scornful faces at me, oppressing me with indescribable horrors.'

Although Hartley didn't socialize with the other boys during the day, he kept them up late, listening to a long, involved tale '. . . night after night, as we lay in bed,' wrote Derwent,

> for a space of years, and not unfrequently for hours together. This enormous romance . . . delivered without premeditation, had a progressive story, with many turns and complications, with salient points recurring at intervals, with a suspended interest varying in intensity, and occasionally wrought up to a very high pitch, and at length a final catastrophe and conclusion . . . There was a great variety of persons sharply characterised, who appeared on stage in combination and not merely in succession . . . He spoke without hesitation, in language as vivid as it was flowing.[15]

When Hartley left school in 1814 at the age of seventeen he was still the odd, imaginative, largely solitary creature (he had, Derwent relates, made only one friend during his schooldays, Robert Jameson) Wordsworth had described eleven years earlier. Accustomed to being treated as a genius, he was also thoroughly undisciplined and haphazardly educated: his knowledge of the classics, for instance, was insufficient for university entry. However, he'd benefited immeasurably from the company he was born

---

14. D. Coleridge (ed.), *Poems of Hartley Coleridge*, p.li.
15. Ibid, pp.liii–liv.

into: 'It was so, rather than by a regular course of study, that he was educated . . . by the living voice of Coleridge, Southey, and Wordsworth, [Charles] Lloyd, [Professor] Wilson, and De Quincey – and again by homely familiarity with town's folk, and country folk, of every degree; lastly, by daily recurring hours of solitude – by lonely wanderings with the murmur of the Brathay in his ear.'[16]

After a period of coaching by Southey[17] – who wrote at the time: 'Hartley's intellect will soon overcome all disadvantages that his exterior may incur, if he do but *keep the course* . . . His disposition is excellent, his principles thoroughly good, and he has instinctively a devotional feeling which I hope will keep them so. An overweening confidence in his own talents, and a perilous habit of finding out reasons for whatever he likes to do, are the dangerous points of his character' – Hartley started at Merton College, Oxford, in 1815.

> My acquaintance with Hartley Coleridge [wrote the Reverend Alexander Dyce to Derwent in July 1849] commenced at Oxford, soon after his first examination in the schools, and it continued till the time when he stood for the Oriel fellowship . . . I remember him only as a young man who possessed an intellect of the highest order, with great simplicity of character, and considerable oddity of manner.
>
> His extraordinary powers as a converser (or rather a declaimer) procured for him numerous invitations to what are called at Oxford 'wine-parties'. He knew that he was

---

16. Ibid, pp.lvi–lvii.
17. Southey also sorted out college entry and raised the money for Hartley's fees, Samuel Taylor Coleridge being, at this time, in no state to take responsibility for organizing, delivering or funding his elder son's education.

expected to talk, and talking was his delight. Leaning his head on one shoulder, turning up his dark bright eyes, and swinging backwards and forwards in his chair, he would hold forth by the hour (for no one wished to interrupt him) on whatever subject might have been started – either of literature, politics, or religion – with an originality of thought, a force of illustration, and a facility and beauty of expression, which I question if any man then living, except his father, could have surpassed.

I have some reason to believe that this display of eloquence did him some harm eventually at the University. Reports were rife that he was fond of inveighing against all establishments . . . and very probably he *had* given cause for such reports being spread abroad by matter-of-fact persons, who could not distinguish between what he said when truth was his sole object, and what he uttered when he was declaiming merely to show his ingenuity in argument. I have little doubt he was no more serious in those supposed 'attacks on Church and State' than he was when he maintained (as I have heard him do) that ages of darkness would again prevail in Europe, to the destruction of literature and the arts . . . or when he gravely asserted that, for all we know, *dogs may have a language of smell*, and that what is to our organs a very disagreeable odour may be to the canine organs *a most beautiful poem*.

It is delightful to me to record such testimony . . . My brother was, however . . . more sincere in his invectives against establishments . . . than Mr. Dyce kindly supposes. Though far from a destructive in politics, he was always keenly alive to what he supposed to be the evils and abuses of the existing state of things both in Church and State . . .[18]

18. D. Coleridge (ed.), *Poems of Hartley Coleridge*, pp.lxiv–lxvi.

Hartley graduated from Merton in 1818, having performed erratically, although well enough to achieve a second-class degree *in literis humanioribus*. He was, as Dyce's account indicates, comparatively happy as an undergraduate; but there was one major upset. He entered his poem 'Horses of Lysippus' for the Newdigate Poetry Prize, expecting to win. And didn't. 'It was', he wrote 'almost the only occasion in my life wherein I was keenly disappointed; for it was the only one upon which I felt any confident hope.'[19] The other reason this failure upset Hartley so much was that winning, he believed, would compensate for his 'diminutive and ungainly exterior', and attract girls. 'I had', he wrote in one of his notebooks, 'an intense and incessant craving for the notice of females, with a foreboding consciousness that I was never fashioned for a ladies' man.'[20]

After graduation, Hartley was offered a fellowship at Oriel College. However, he failed his probationary year, through behaving in a way his employers felt to be deeply inappropriate. Amongst other charges, he was accused of excessive social drinking, anti-authoritarianism, inept timekeeping, consorting with the wrong type of person (i.e. anyone who wasn't an Oriel fellow) and not shaving often enough. Whilst all this might have constituted a conscious rebellion, Oriel was a particularly austere and regimented place, and it's just as plausible to suggest that the undisciplined, open-hearted, congenitally odd but brilliant Hartley simply wasn't capable of fitting in. 'To tell the truth,' he wrote in a letter to Derwent, May 1821, 'I did not much like the state of a probationer, or submit, as I ought to have

19. Ibid, p.lxxxiii.
20. Ibid, pp.lxxxiv–lxxxv.

done, to a yoke of observances which I sincerely think very absurd . . .'[21]

Yet he was devastated by the rejection. As was his father: considerable attempts were made by STC and others to get Hartley reinstated, but ultimately the family accepted £300 compensation from the college. And this failure at Oriel both coloured and set the tone for the rest of Hartley's life.

In 1820 Hartley moved to London, hoping – optimistically – to earn his living by writing. He produced a few short poems and essays for the *London* magazine, and wrote (but never finished) *Prometheus*. Derwent tells us that he intended to do much more, including a prose translation of Aeschylus' plays. But by now his habitual procrastination had kicked in and, after a couple of years, STC insisted he return to the Lakes, and take a position as schoolmaster. Hartley was reluctant and wrote to his father:

> *I felt a physical incapacity of exerting the necessary authority, and preserving the necessary distance among a set of boys, in whose number there must needs be found high spirits and intractable natures. Boys of fifteen are harder to govern than men of twenty, and yet I can sincerely say I did my utmost at Oxford to perform the duties of a tutor, and I did it in vain . . . It is my wish to make another trial of my talents in London. I know I can make more than a livelihood, and I have hopes – more than hopes – of my own steady perseverance in the right path; but I will not be obstinate. Only let me say – that, what with my past failures, what with the unavoidable weakness of nerves, and defect of that sort of*

---

21. Ibid, p.lxxxviii.

sternness which is a necessary supplement to kindness in a pedagogue, I think schooling, of all things possible, the least eligible.[22]

In 1823, however, Hartley acceded to his father's wishes and returned to Ambleside, taking over when his former schoolmaster, Mr Dawes, retired. He seemed to settle, but was scared of his pupils and couldn't maintain discipline. Within a few years, the school he ran with a more dynamic colleague, Mr Stuart, had failed, mostly because Stuart, banking on the Coleridge name, had expanded the enterprise too ambitiously, but also partly because Hartley's terrified ineptitude lost them pupils.

A few years after the school closed, Hartley explained himself in a letter to his mother:

For all the duties of preceptor, except the simple communication of knowledge, I am as physically unfitted as dear papa for those of a horse-soldier. For a teacher who has to deal with females or young men, it may be sufficient if you can engage attention; but the master of school-boys must be able to command it, and this is a faculty not to be acquired. It depends upon the voice, the eye, and the nerve. Every hour that I spent with my pupils was passed in a state more nearly related to fear than to anything else. How, then, could I endure to be among unruly boys from seven in the morning till eight or nine at night, to be responsible for actions which I could no more control than I could move a pyramid? Strange it may be, but I have an instinctive horror of big boys – perhaps derived from the persecution which I suffered from them when a little one.[23]

---

22. Ibid, p.xciv.
23. Ibid, p.xcviii.

Next, Hartley moved to Grasmere, where he lived first at an inn, then with an elderly widow, Mrs Fleming, who looked after him affectionately. When she died, her house and tenant were taken over by William and Eleanor Richardson. They also adored Hartley, and then took him with them to Nab Cottage in Rydal when they moved there. Years later, Canon Rawnsley reported his conversations with William: 'His eyes would almost fill with tears as he spoke of Hartley's end. "Ya kna," he would say, "Lile Hartley was as manashable as a bairn, and was a bairn that needed manashing until the end." '[24]

After a brief sojourn in Leeds in the early 1830s, working for a publisher called Bingley – who employed Hartley to write brief biographies of famous northern men,[25] brought out the only volume of Hartley's poetry published in the poet's lifetime, and then went bankrupt in 1833 – Hartley spent the rest of his life living in the Lake District. He wrote occasionally for magazines, composed a great deal of verse, and hung out with the locals. He never managed to earn enough money to keep himself but, as he lived frugally, never proved a huge burden to his family, who were happy to provide financial assistance. He would disappear periodically, spend weeks living rough, and would eventually be found in an inn, where, according to Rawnsley, he might pay for his drink 'by the singing of his favourite song, "The Tortoise-shell Cat," or by the making of an eloquent speech on national or local matters.'[26]

Derwent wrote:

---

24. H. D. Rawnsley, *Literary Associations of the English Lakes*, vol.II, pp.138–9.
25. First published as *Biographia Borealis*, later as *The Lives of the Northern Worthies*.
26. H. D. Rawnsley, *Literary Associations of the English Lakes*, vol.II, p.97.

His time was spent much as it had been when he was a boy, out of doors in lonely reverie, in intercourse with his many friends, or at his desk; for though he read much, it was commonly with the pen in his hand.

As I have before intimated, his purposeless wanderings had been sometimes pursued till he lost the power to return . . . He could not fall among strangers. Go where he would, be where he might, he was treated with affectionate respect. Love followed him like his shadow . . . Among his friends we must count men, women, and children, of every rank and every age . . . In the farmhouse or the cottage, not alone at times of rustic festivity at a sheep-shearing, a wedding, or a christening, but by the ingle side with the grandmother or the 'bairns,' he was made, and felt himself, at home . . . He would nurse an infant by the hour. A like overflowing of his affectionate nature was seen in his fondness for animals – for anything that would love him in return – simply, and for its own sake, rather than for his.[27]

During 1837 and 1838 he helped out in a couple of local schools, proving a more successful teacher when faced with classes of boys who were already disciplined and motivated. Thomas Blackburne – a pupil who became a close friend of Hartley's – recalled:

Out of school he never mixed with the boys, but was sometimes seen, to their astonishment, running along the fields with his arms outstretched, and talking to himself . . . His enthusiasm carried him off the rails. His genius was too uneven to run in a groove, his conversation was a continual

_____

27. D. Coleridge, *Poems of Hartley Coleridge*, pp.cxxiv–cxxvi.

sparkle; very irregular and unequal, yet, when worked up to a certain warmth, throwing out jets and gushes so radiant and hilarious that, like a Christmas fire, it inspirited and made happy everybody . . .

On his way to . . . [a party] . . . he called on me, and I could not help saying, 'How well you look in a white neck-cloth!' 'I wish you could see me sometimes,' he replied; 'if I had only black-silk stockings and shoe-buckles I should be quite a gentleman.' Those who had only seen him in the careless dress that he chose to adopt in the lanes – his trowsers, which were generally too long, doubled half way up the leg, unbrushed, and often splashed; his hat brushed the wrong way, for he never used an umbrella; and his wild, unshaven, weather-beaten look – were amazed at his meta-morphose into such a faultless gentleman as he appeared when he was dressed for the evening.[28]

'I have known him', recalled another friend, 'enter into metaphys-ical disquisitions with a Cumberland peasant . . . or deliver what might be called an historical lecture to a group of Cumberland farmers . . . Their respect for his talents amounted to veneration . . . but, more than this, he was deeply beloved amongst them. I have heard some of that class say, they would "go through fire and water for Mr. Coleridge".'[29]

Others, however, reported less positively. Charles Cox, in his essay 'Harriette Harrison's Grasmere Journal', quotes the govern-ess, holidaying in the Lakes from Bury during summer 1847:

. . . when just ready for a walk, Margaret . . . said Mr. Coleridge was at the door. Of course he was to be asked in,

---

28. Ibid, pp.cxxxii–cxxxvi.
29. Ibid, p.cxxxi.

but as Mr. Grundy was not anxious to spend a second long evening with him, it was agreed that we should stroll about until Mr. O. had despatched his visitor, whom he was enjoined to offer *no wine* or *gin*.

The previous night, Harriette had asked Hartley the publication date of Samuel Taylor Coleridge's *Table Talk*. Hartley had returned with a letter containing the answer, which also mentioned that this very day – 25th July – marked exactly thirteen years since Samuel Taylor Coleridge had died. 'On this anniversary of that Father's death, whose loss his pen had only an hour before so feelingly deplored, did he after asking for brandy under plea of toothache become so intoxicated as to be scarcely able to walk . . .'[30]

One of the most vivid descriptions of Hartley Coleridge in later life comes from *The Recollections of Aubrey de Vere*, the STC enthusiast, poet and author who met him during a trip to the Lakes in 1844.

> One day Miss Fenwick drove me to Nab Cottage, just under Rydal Mount, near Rydal Water, and the residence of Hartley Coleridge. She sent for him, and at once he was with us. It was a white-haired apparition – wearing in all other aspects the semblance of youth – with the most delicately-grained and tinted skin and vividly bright eyes. He could hardly be said to have walked, for he seemed with difficulty to keep his feet on the ground, as he wavered near us with arms extended like wings. Everything that he said was strange and quaint, whilst perfectly unaffected, and, though always amusing, yet always represented a mind whose thoughts dwelt in a region

---

30. Published in *The Wordsworth Circle*, vol.11, no.4, autumn 1980.

as remote as the antipodes. After fifty years of ill-fortune the man before us was still the child described by Wordsworth in his poem to 'H. C. at three [sic] years old.'

. . . A few days later he dined with us . . . It was a strange thing to see Hartley Coleridge fluctuating about the room, now with one hand on his head, now with both arms expanded like a swimmer's. There was some element wanting in his being. He could do everything but keep his footing, and doubtless in his inner world of thought, it was easier for him to fly than to walk, to walk than to stand. There seemed to be no gravitating principle in him. One might have thought he needed stones in his pockets to prevent his being blown away. But he is said to have always lived 'an innocent life, though far astray', and he might, perhaps, have been more easily changed into an angel than into a simply strong man.[31]

Some years after Hartley's death, Canon Rawnsley, interviewing Lakesmen for anecdotes about Wordsworth would be informed that 'But he wasn't a man as was thowte a deal o' for his potry when he was hereabout. It hed no laugh in it same as Lile Hartley's, bided a deal o makkin I darsay.'[32] Hartley's, in contrast, 'was made up as he trotted along by the brooks', was 'popped down upo' paper at the first open door, and was gaily well liket by a vast of fowk cracking over a pint of yaale'. 'Cliverest man i' England as some say, and did a deal to help Mr. Wudsworth out with his potry and all.'[33]

But Hartley loved Wordsworth's poetry, and he and the poet loved each other. When Hartley died, Wordsworth was 'deeply

31. Aubrey de Vere, *Recollections of Aubrey de Vere*, pp.133–5.
32. H. D. Rawnsley, *Literary Associations of the English Lakes* vol.II, p.137
33. Ibid, vol.II, pp.138–9.

affected', according to Derwent, 'having desired the sexton to measure out the ground for his own and for Mrs. Wordsworth's grave ... bade him measure out the space of a third grave ... immediately beyond' for Hartley. '"Let him lie by us," Wordsworth said. "He would have wished it." '[34]

---

34. D. Coleridge (ed.), *Poems of Hartley Coleridge*, pp.clxxxv–clxxxvi.